VENICE

VENICE

THE CHURCH OF ST. MARK'S
THE TREASURE OF ST. MARK'S
THE DUCAL PALACE
THE GALLERIE DELL'ACCADEMIA
THE ARCHITECTURE AND MONUMENTS OF VENICE

TEXT BY

MICHELANGELO MURARO
*formerly of the Superintendence of Monuments in Venice
now of the Superintendence of Monuments in Florence*

AND

ANDRÉ GRABAR
Professor at the Collège de France in Paris

PORTLAND HOUSE
NEW YORK

© 1986 by Editions d'Art Albert Skira S.A., Geneva, Switzerland

First edition 1963

This edition published in 1987 by Portland House,
distributed by Crown Publishers, Inc.,
225 Park Avenue South, New York, New York 10003

ISBN 0-517-62645-4

Printed and bound in Switzerland

h g f e d c b a

CONTENTS

THE MYTH OF VENICE

THE GRIMANI "ABUNDANCE." GREEK STATUE OF THE SECOND HALF OF THE FIFTH CENTURY B.C. MARBLE. ARCHAEOLOGICAL MUSEUM.

I

THE MYTH OF VENICE

In 1222 Doge Pietro Ziani, speaking before the Senate, proposed that Venice should be abandoned and the Venetian capital transferred to Constantinople. It was not, as in the legends of other ancient peoples, that the Doge was obeying the dictates of a voice from heaven. On the contrary, his proposal was prompted by considerations of a purely practical order. Constantinople had been conquered and occupied in 1203 by the Crusaders, an enterprise in which Venice, under the great Doge Enrico Dandolo, played a leading part. Thus was founded the Latin Empire of the East (1204-1261) and Constantinople, its capital, became the foremost commercial metropolis of the world. Large numbers of the boldest, most enterprising citizens had therefore moved from Venice to Constantinople, which was the terminus of the great caravan route from the East and the point of departure of all the trade routes westward. Venice, in comparison, occupied a geographical position far removed from the centre of affairs; standing moreover on a site laboriously wrested from the sea, she was surrounded by waters and marshlands which might at any moment engulf her, as they had already engulfed two island towns of the Lagoon, Ammiana and Costanziaca. The proposal of Pietro Ziani was discussed and debated at length in the Venetian Senate. In the end, we read, it was vetoed by a single vote—that, as legend has it, of Angelo Falier.

This, like other legends connected with her early history, goes far to illuminate the character and destiny of Venice. It may therefore be worth while to interpret and evaluate, if we can, the significance of this episode, particularly striking in the bold and ready spirit of adventure to which it testifies. Ancient poets, in describing a merchant, pictured him as busily and vigilantly superintending his affairs aboard ship. For the sea was thought of as the natural element of one who earned his livelihood by trade. Of the Venetians it was said: *"Proficuum et honorem Venetiarum eundo et redeundo"* (Their goings and comings make the wealth and honour of the Venetians). So that the audacious proposal of Doge Ziani need not surprise us coming from a

Venetian. It would not have been the first time that the Venetian people emigrated *en masse*. In the beginning, fleeing before invaders who were overrunning the North Italian mainland, they loaded boats and rafts with their families and working implements, with wood and stones suitable for house-building, and made for the shoals and sand banks in the Lagoon. First they settled in the neighbourhood of Heraclea. Then, finding the place too far from the open sea, they again took to their boats, with their families and all their belongings, and moved to Malamocco, on the opposite side of the Lagoon. From there they had free access to the Adriatic and began trading in salt and fish with the towns on the neighbouring shores. But when in time Malamocco proved to be difficult to defend, being too much exposed to enemy attack, they had no hesitation about withdrawing to safer ground. This time they chose the Rialtine islands, half way between the mainland and the open sea; there, centred at Rialto, they made their permanent home. Under Doge Agnello Partecipazio (811-827) was built the city that was to become the Venice we know today. Heraclea and Malamocco, each in turn chosen as the capital, only to be abandoned, gradually sank back into the silence and stagnation of the Lagoon. Such would have been the fate of Venice herself, had the deciding vote of Angelo Falier not saved her from abandonment and oblivion.

The party of Pietro Ziani represented the bold, adventurous spirit of the merchants and seafarers. The opposing party, that of Angelo Falier, represented another, equally forcible aspect of the Venetian character: attachment to the past and fidelity to tradition—qualities which here assumed the value of an ideal and a guarantee of the binding power of commitments and contracts. It was a matter of policy in Venice never to revoke a law that had proved its effectiveness, never to change institutions of government and commerce that had proved their worth. Privileges and prerogatives once established, and agreements and promises once made, became sacred and had to be respected. Venetian ducats alone, of all the currency used in Europe in the Middle Ages, never changed in weight or value. Hence the stability of the Venetian government, and the renown it enjoyed on the strength of its incorruptible probity and political wisdom.

On the corner of the Ducal Palace nearest the sea—where it met the eyes of Venetian sailors on their return from war and trading ventures—the same myth was twice represented, symbolizing the love of one's parents and kinsmen: Noah's son covering the Patriarch in his nakedness, and Tobias, attended by the Angel, with the fish whose gall was miraculously to cure his father's blindness.

Unable to believe that their forefathers had miscalculated in settling permanently in the islands of the Lagoon, the Venetians could not bring themselves to forsake their city and their homes for a distant capital in a foreign land, in a different climate, amid strange peoples and customs, however alluring might be the promise of wealth and empire that it held out.

But if the party of Angelo Falier prevailed and the Venetians were deterred from abandoning their island city, it was chiefly for moral and religious reasons. There was an old tradition in the Middle Ages among the peoples of the Upper Adriatic, that St Mark the Evangelist, on his way to preach the Faith in Aquileia, was caught in a violent storm and driven to land on a deserted island of the Lagoon. There, during his sleep, an angel appeared to him, saying, *"Pax tibi, Marce, Evangelista meus"* (Peace to thee, Mark my Evangelist), and announced that one day his body should find a resting place and veneration on that very island. Each settlement in the Lagoon thereafter claimed the promised privilege for its own island and looked forward to its realization. Venice, opportune as always in her decisions to act, secured the relics of the Saint in 828, thus fulfilling the prophecy which gave to her, and her alone, authority and dominion over all her rivals. The legend at this point becomes so detailed and circumstantial as to read like a true account of actual events. The daring enterprise was led by two Venetian merchants, Messer Rustico of Torcello and Messer Buono of Malamocco. As their ship lay at Alexandria (then in the hands of the Infidels), they succeeded in bringing away the body of St Mark from the church where it was enshrined and returned with it to Venice. St Mark thus found his last resting place in Venice and became the patron saint of the city.

Two centuries later a further episode in the legend of St Mark was enacted in circumstances that were never to be forgotten. Lest some rival city should attempt to steal the relics of the Saint, they were secretly consigned to a hiding place known only to the Doge and the Primicerius, the leading ecclesiastical dignitary. A day came, however—perhaps in the time of the popular uprising against Pietro Candiano—when both the Doge and the Primicerius died before they were able to transmit the great secret to their successors. Great was the consternation at the loss of the relics. Solemn fasts and processions were held; prostrate in the church (as shown in one of the mosaics in St Mark's), the people prayed for a miracle and implored the Saint to reveal himself. Their prayers were answered and a miracle occurred. On the 25th of June, 1094, a great light shone down in the church, part of the masonry gave way, and a hand was thrust out—the body had been found. St Mark, patron and defender of the city, had come back among the Venetians.

Here, for the first time, we find current in Venice a myth deriving from ancient Rome. Venerated on the Palatine Hill was a black stone covering the entrance to the world of the gods and Penates; this *lapis niger* was regarded as the central point of the city and the very centre of the world. For the Venetians too, past and present, divine and human, all found their central point of being in a particular place: the pillar in the church of St Mark's where the Evangelist's relics had been hidden. The miracle of their rediscovery was commemorated by an oil lamp burning day and night and the image of a warrior saint, the archangel Michael, painted on the marble slab of the pillar. It was on this consecrated spot that the Doge, immediately after his election, was presented to the people. After his miraculous apparition there could be no doubt as to the living presence of the Saint; that presence confirmed the special protection accorded by St Mark to the Venetian people, and the sanctity of the place in which they worshipped him.

But in addition to the religious associations which bound the Venetians to their city, there were other motives, perhaps even more deep-seated though less explicit, that weighed heavily in the balance and persuaded them to remain where they were. They could not forget that the islands on which they lived had once been barren shoals, that their city and their very homes had been built up from nothing; every stone had a history of its own that spoke directly to the heart of a Venetian. The earliest settlers had lived precariously in their boats and in wattled huts; to build houses and churches, stone, tools and virtually all the necessaries of life had to be brought from the mainland. The slow task of accumulation went forward day by day—a task of infinite patience which Herman Melville has compared to that of the coral-producing insects of the atolls in the South Seas. Venice was the devoted handiwork of untold generations, and the Venetians could never forget it. It was asking too much that they should now uproot themselves and hazard all on a wild scheme of empire in the East. What their fathers had accomplished, against the inhospitable elements, was not only a treasured patrimony but a guarantee of safety. Thus in the early ninth century, when the Frankish king Pepin moved up his fleet against the city, the Venetians in their light craft lured his heavy vessels into the swamps at high tide and, when they were left high and dry, easily defeated them.

By 1222 the vicissitudes of Venice's early history were over, and her institutions had been stabilized. By now her face was turned towards Europe and even her physical aspect had become definitely Western. The experience of many centuries had borne fruit. Already the city presented itself to the eye as a kind of palimpsest in which the observer might recognize all the strata of the successive cultures that had flourished on the islands in the early centuries of their history. From every country with which she had come in contact Venice had borrowed whatever might serve her turn. Although she seemed insatiable in her acquisitiveness, and took readily from all without distinction of race or creed, yet her growth and evolution followed an organic logic which led her to weave a network of relationships with distant lands and above all with peoples who, though famous for old-established cultures of their own, had entered on a decline.

This famous cameo, one of the masterpieces of ancient glyptic art, was discovered in the ruins of Ephesus and acquired at Smyrna in the eighteenth century by Girolamo Zulian. "Aegis Bearer" is one of the epithets applied to Zeus in Homer; the "aegis" was the shield or buckler fashioned for Zeus by Hephaestus (Vulcan). So highly valued was this cameo that in the Napoleonic era, when it was taken away to Paris, the Venetians, in order to get it back, gave a large number of illuminated manuscripts in exchange for it.

BUST OF ZEUS THE AEGIS BEARER, KNOWN AS THE ZULIAN CAMEO. HELLENISTIC ART. SARDONYX IN TWO LAYERS. ARCHAEOLOGICAL MUSEUM.

Founded a short distance from the ancient Spina, which in early times had been an important terminus on the trade routes linking Central Europe with the Mediterranean, Venice owed its existence to the fact that, in an emergency, the lagoon islands answered a definite purpose: they provided a safe place of refuge for the peoples of the neighbouring mainland, driven from their homes by the barbarian invasions that put an end to the Roman Empire.

Never having recognized the authority of the Huns or Lombards, and remaining undefeated and uninvaded amid the protecting waters of the Lagoon, the Venetians continued to regard themselves as Roman citizens. And in emulation of Roman ideals they developed into a well-organized community independent and practical in its outlook, law-abiding, open-minded and empirical, with a strong sense of social cohesion. In Venice, as in Rome, the law and the exigencies of the common weal were more binding than blood relationships and family ties, and Venetian citizenship was open to foreigners who for a stipulated length of time had made their home in the city. Venetian institutions, traditions, legends, even the Venetian mentality, were in many ways reminiscent of Rome. The pillar in St Mark's, where the miraculous recovery of the Saint's relics took place, was to the Venetians what the *lapis niger* was to the Romans. To the Rape of the Sabine Women corresponds a similar incident in the early history of Venice: the legend of the Venetian brides carried off by Istrian pirates. Public offices and the hierarchy of the state were Latin in character and given Latin names. The Doge himself, as Chief of State, took his title from the Latin *dux*, meaning leader or military commander; and, in imitation of ancient prerogatives, he also had authority over the church, though he never achieved the dignity of Pontifex Maximus. The Venetian year, like the Roman year, began in March.

It was her steadfast fidelity to Roman ways and ideals that enabled Venice to survive the political crises of the Middle Ages, and the Roman example made a profound and lasting impress on the art and manners of the city. Leading Venetian families contrived to trace their ancestry to ancient Rome, and poets and historians described Venice as the "New Rome." This strong sense of the past, characteristic of the Venetians, led them to form collections of antiquities and classical art, for they had been accustomed from the earliest times to seeing ancient stones and carvings embedded in the very walls of their houses. Though there were few traces of Roman history in the Lagoon itself, the neighbouring towns of the mainland, like Altino and Aquileia (whence many Venetian families originated), were rich in Roman monuments and remains. It was

The Archaeological Museum of Venice originated in 1523 when Cardinal Domenico Grimani bequeathed his collection of ancient marbles and bronzes to the Venetian government. In 1586 it was substantially increased by the donations of his nephew, Giovanni Grimani, which included both this pagan altar with erotic reliefs and the fine statue of Persephone personifying Abundance (reproduced on page 8); the latter is one of the very few original pieces of Greek sculpture to come down to us from the time of Pheidias.

THE GRIMANI ALTAR: SATYR AND MAENAD EMBRACING (LEFT) AND SATYR DANCING TO THE HARP PLAYED BY A MAENAD (RIGHT). HELLENISTIC ART OF THE SECOND CENTURY B.C. MARELE. ARCHAEOLOGICAL MUSEUM.

her fidelity to Rome, moreover, that led Venice to take one of the most momentous decisions in her history. By recognizing the Byzantine Emperor as the legitimate successor of the ancient Roman Emperors, and submitting to his authority, Venice made it clear that she meant to hold aloof from feudal Europe. She thus maintained her independence with respect to the continent, turning for support to the Eastern capital, inheritor of the prestige and authority of Ancient Rome.

Of all the cultural strata underlying the formation of modern Venice, the Byzantine contribution is probably the one that has remained most substantial and enduring. The most eloquent memorial of her submission to Byzantium is of course the church of St Mark's, built in a style which, running counter to every local tradition, clearly demonstrated where the allegiance of the Venetians lay. But their open declaration of allegiance to Byzantium did not correspond to exigencies of a spiritual order alone; there were also practical reasons for it. The remoteness of the imperial capital, and the instability of the Exarchate of Ravenna representing the authority of the Byzantine emperor in Italy, were so many guarantees that Venice, though nominally a vassal, would remain in actual practice an independent State.

The fact of maintaining close ties with so distant a capital had a further effect on the national character: it greatly broadened the Venetians' outlook, particularly in comparison with the narrow, static horizons of the mainland towns around the Lagoon. As she plied the trade routes of the East, and grew and prospered, Venice gradually extended the privileges obtained from the Byzantine emperors. In all their ports of call, ships flying the flag of San Marco were granted customs facilities even greater than those enjoyed by the Byzantines themselves. Everything conspired to draw the Venetians eastward; not commercial interests only, but the pomp and ceremony of the Court of Constantinople, whose splendour and fascination far outshone anything then to be found in the lands of the West. There the Doges sent their sons to be educated; from thence came the best artists and the finest works of religious art, like the great altar screen known as the Pala d'Oro, which was ordered from Constantinople at some time between 976 and the year 1000. Even Byzantine coins were for many centuries imitated by the Venetians.

While France too had contacts with Byzantium, it was always by way of Venice. And if certain architectural forms, taken over from the Byzantines, flourished anew in the Europe of the Renaissance, it was because Venice had kept them alive and was able to hand them down to modern times. Even today the name of many a *calle* and many a *piazza* in Venice has Byzantine associations. It was in accordance with a Byzantine tradition that Venetian churches were dedicated to Old Testament prophets like Jeremiah (San Geremia) and Zechariah (San Zaccaria). Typically Byzantine too was the Venetian love of colour, which found expression in mosaics and in buildings faced with polychrome marbles.

BRONZE HORSES. ROMAN ART OF THE FIRST CENTURY B.C. LOGGIA OF ST MARK'S, OVER THE MAIN ENTRANCE.

These four horses are the only quadriga of classical antiquity still in existence. In the early Middle Ages they stood on the towers of the hippodrome in Constantinople; after the sack of the city by the Crusaders in 1203, they were shipped to Venice, where they came to be regarded as the symbol of Venetian power. After the fall of the Republic in 1797, Napoleon had them taken down and sent to Paris to adorn the Arc du Carrousel. Brought back to Venice in 1815, they were restored to their old position on the open platform or loggia over the atrium of St Mark's (where they can be seen in Gentile Bellini's painting reproduced on page 144). Visible above, on the right, are Sansovino's Libreria Vecchia and the Campanile.

Wholly dependent on overseas trade, the Venetians learned to look about them with a sharp eye and were quick to take advantage of favourable circumstances. Their contacts with the Arab world, for example, proved to be particularly fruitful. Experienced sailors and traders, maintaining commercial relations with the most distant peoples of Asia, the Arabs had passed their zenith and were moving towards their decline by the time Venetian merchant ships appeared in the Eastern Mediterranean. And since the Infidels were denied access to the countries of the Christian hinterland, the Venetians made themselves indispensable as middlemen in the buying and selling of textiles, glassware, leather and wrought metals. Christian pilgrims from all over Europe bound for the Holy Land had no choice but to take passage on Venetian ships, which alone sailed under the protection of special safe-conducts issued by the Infidels. A *chanson de geste* of the cycle of Guillaume d'Orange (about 1275) sings of an imagined Venice conquered by the Arabs and governed by a Sultan named Brunamont; a Christian hero, Renier, sets the city free, marries the Sultan's daughter, and Venice reverts to Christianity.

Even today it is easy to see how deep was the Arab and Moorish influence on the architecture and life of the city. "Before passing into the hands of the Venetians," writes Henri Pirenne, "Mediterranean trade was controlled from Baghdad." And, as Ruskin observed, the Venetians found it natural to imitate the elegant details of Arab houses. Copings and domes, decorations and polychrome inlays, gardens and courtyards, the love of vegetation, of fountains and pools, of all that brightens and beautifies life—these things the Venetians and the Arabs had in common. An inscription on the walls of the Alhambra describes an ideal city which one is tempted to identify with Venice. "Its shores, beyond the expanse of waters, are works of art carved in the choicest marble. The solid element and the waters, the marbles and the fluid element, blend together in the vision: of the two, which is it that flows?"

Of the many chapters of Venetian history that remain to be written, one of the most interesting, certainly, is that of its relations with the Arabs and Turks. The Serene Republic styled herself the "Bastion of the Faith," the defender of Christianity. Yet all the evidence goes to show that the Venetians remained on good terms with the Infidels—from the repeated threats of Pope and Emperor against the Venetians for doing business with them, to the recorded presence of Arab artisans in the city, where they were employed not only in the Arsenal but also, it would seem, in St Mark's

This is but one detail of a vast floor mosaic (measuring 121 by 59 feet) executed for Bishop Theodore, who died about A.D. 320. The scenes represented allude to the triumph and peace achieved by the Church after the Edict of Milan (313). Jonah's escape from the fish was regarded as prefiguring the Resurrection of Christ. The Orant figure in the boat, on the left, links this Old Testament scene with the Christian dispensation and represents the priest praying for the salvation of the people.

JONAH THROWN OVERBOARD AND SWALLOWED BY A FISH. EARLY CHRISTIAN ART OF THE FOURTH CENTURY.
FLOOR MOSAIC, CATHEDRAL OF AQUILEIA.

MEDALLION WITH THE LAMB, UPHELD BY FOUR ANGELS. RAVENNATE ART OF THE SEVENTH CENTURY.
MOSAIC IN THE RIGHTHAND APSE, CATHEDRAL OF SANTA MARIA ASSUNTA, TORCELLO.

The high quality of the mosaic work, together with the style and iconography, show this to be a very early work, attributable to the period when, as recorded in an ancient commemorative tablet, the church was founded (630) "in the reign of the Emperor Heraclius by order of the exarch and patrician Isaac." At that time a populous and flourishing community, Torcello became the seat of a bishop (638) and the residence of the first Doge of Venice (697). Today the island is all but deserted, though its principal monuments remain: the eleventh-century church of Santa Fosca and the still older cathedral of Santa Maria Assunta with its great mosaics.

itself. As regards the Venetian trading colonies, Ruskin wrote (in *St Mark's Rest*):
"Whether they were in Asia, Africa, or the Island of Atlantis, did not at this time
greatly matter; but it mattered infinitely that they were colonies living in friendly
relations with the Saracen." The most striking example of the material advantages
gained by conciliating the Infidels is to be found in the relations of Venice with Egypt.
By allying herself with the Moslems who had swept across North Africa, she was
able to secure many valuable relics formerly in the possession of the Copts, including
the relics of St Mark the Evangelist, who before becoming the patron saint of Venice
had been that of Alexandria. The connections between the two cities were close,
and indeed there were even affinities of character between them. What the Emperor
Hadrian had once said of Alexandria, that "no one lives in idleness there," also held
good for Venice; and of the Venetians, as of the Alexandrians, it might have been
said that they worshipped but one god: money. As international as Alexandria
(where, wrote St John Chrysostom, Greeks, Italians, Libyans, Cilicians, Arabs,
Indians and Scyths met and mingled), Venice owed some of her most thriving indus-
tries to that ancient emporium—her trade in precious objects for both secular and
liturgical use, for example. But it was the religious heritage that proved most valuable
of all. Stripped of her wealth and prestige, Alexandria passed on to Venice the very
thing she needed in order to break free of Byzantium and assert her independence:
the patriarchal title and religious authority of St Mark the Evangelist, her new patron
saint who supplanted the Greek saint Theodore and whose coming introduced in
Venice a less aulic, less abstract form of worship. The opportunity of asserting her
independence came with the proclamation of Iconoclasm, which the Venetians
resolutely opposed, determined as they were to preserve in their churches the images
venerated by their ancestors—an attitude prophetic of the rich flowering of the
figurative arts in Venice in later times.

So far we have spoken only of the earliest time-layers which went to form the great
palimpsest of Venice—those of the Romans, the Byzantines, the Greeks, the Arabs,
the Copts. Since each of these civilizations has left in the Lagoon a deposit of characteristic works, we have made a point of illustrating some of the most significant among
them in order to show the rich and varied cultural background out of which Venice
may be said to have grown and taken form. For centuries Venice accumulated works
of art created elsewhere, as yet unable to produce anything in the way of original art.
Nor could this be otherwise until the focus of her efforts was concentrated, not on
cultures remote in time and place, but on the present exigencies of her own cultural
development. The first tokens of a genuinely Venetian art are probably some of the
Romanesque protomes supporting the cornices of the galleries in St Mark's. The initial
stimulus came from Verona, which supplied Venice with marble and grain—as appears
from many extant documents recording payments in Veronese currency. But the great
step forward, towards power and independence, came with the Crusades and the
influx of French culture into the lagoons.

On December 20, 1203, the Crusaders entered Constantinople as conquerors and Venice, as the faithful ally of the French, now enjoyed her greatest triumph: she had subdued and occupied the ancient capital of the East, Byzantium, which for centuries had nominally been her overlord and, at times, a thorn in her side. From that day the French language and French manners became fashionable in Venice, and France set the standards of art and taste. But now, unlike her practice in the past, Venice did not simply borrow and appropriate: there was in the arts the same give-and-take, as between equally matched partners, as in the field of war and politics. It was now that Venice began to display her creative powers and her originality.

The history of Venice is henceforth that of a great power, and one whose interests and course of development, let it be said at once, by no means always coincided with those of the rest of Italy. Hence the necessity of considering Venice, and judging her, as an independent entity. Ruskin divided her history into four distinct periods, "four ages," as he called them, distinguished "by the changes in the chief element of every nation's mind—its religion, with the consequent results upon its art." But as regards Venice it seems inadvisable to lay so much stress on the metaphysical element of her character and make-up. Our aim here has been rather to focus attention on a few key points, on certain landmarks in her growth and history, signalized periodically by far-sighted decisions of policy which, in the result, reoriented and reshaped the life and art of the city.

The first such step was taken in the very beginning when the barbarian invaders were defied and the inhabitants of the Lagoon entrenched themselves in their islands, defending their independence against all comers. This early period is marked by many stratagems and bold decisions, which say much for the vitality and resourcefulness of the islanders. But intent as they were on welding themselves into an organized and unified community capable of survival, on building their houses, on acquiring the necessities and a few of the ornaments of life, the early Venetians could not be expected to display any particular originality in the arts. They accumulated objects of every kind; they appreciated and acquired the products of other cultures, but had as yet none of their own. Venetian culture, properly speaking, may be said to begin in the time of Doge Sebastiano Ziani (1172-1178), which initiates the second stage in the rise of the Venetian Republic.

Venice, at this time, can scarcely be said to have any definable boundaries. As fluid as the watery element from which she sprang, she ranged far and wide, restless, uncontainable, insatiably acquisitive. But the outlines of her commercial empire had come to assume a definite form. Venice no longer did business piecemeal, at haphazard, through the medium of isolated traders; she was now a nation of merchants bound by common interests, protected by agreements and treaties, and co-ordinated by the authority of the Consul representing the Venetian government wherever, in foreign

AN EMPEROR OF THE EAST. BYZANTINE RELIEF OF THE TENTH CENTURY.
MARBLE MEDALLION ON THE FAÇADE OF HOUSE NO. 3717, CAMPIELLO ANGARAN, VENICE.

ports and marts, a Venetian community was established. Venice had initiative and
organizing power enough to overcome all competitors among the seafaring nations.
As she thus rose to the height of her wealth and prosperity, she definitely threw in her
lot with the West, embracing French culture and joining the French in the conquest of
Constantinople in the Fourth Crusade. From these endeavours, and this deployment of
energy, emerged at last an art peculiarly Venetian. As might have been expected, it
combined a wonderful variety of basic elements: French and Romanesque influences,
Byzantine gravity, the shifting patterns of Arab art, Germanic harshness, and the
archaism of certain anachronistic forms. But the amalgamation was successful and all

these elements were fused and unified. So strong was the art impulse of fourteenth-century Venice that it revitalized the Gothic style, enriching it with Moslem elements and recasting its forms to suit the traditions and setting of the lagoon city. The result was a style, distinct from any other, which can only be described as Venetian Gothic.

In the course of the fourteenth and fifteenth centuries the face of the city underwent a gradual but almost total change. The Romanesque-Byzantine structures of earlier times were gradually covered over with Gothic ornaments, while the public buildings and private palaces erected now, and they were many, were all in the new Venetian Gothic style.

Thus did Venice bring herself up to date, nor could she have done otherwise, living as she did in constant contact with all the countries and markets of Europe. By availing herself of ancient privileges and unscrupulous methods, however, in her dealings with others, the Serene Republic alienated her neighbours and competitors, until a day came when she found herself encircled by enemies. Led by the Genoese, those enemies slowly closed in on her, reaching the very shores of the Lagoon and occupying Chioggia, only eighteen miles from Venice. Already the Genoese admiral Paganino Doria was boasting that he would soon bit and bridle the four bronze horses of St Mark's, which in foreign eyes symbolized the imperial ambitions of Venice. But the Venetians were indomitable: they succeeded in turning the tables on the besieging Genoese and decisively defeated them (1380). "Thus closed the famous war of Chioggia, the acutest crisis through which the Republic ever passed" (Horatio F. Brown). But Venice issued from the war much weakened. In subscribing to the Peace of Turin (1381), which stripped her of many of her possessions, she manfully accepted the inevitable and looked to the future to mend her fortunes.

Now begins a third period in Venetian history. The first had been marked by the indiscriminate accumulation of materials required to support life in the lagoons, and to enhance it; the second, by the development of Venetian Gothic. The keynote this time was the rise of Renaissance art. To understand how it was that so many Tuscan masters came to Venice in the fifteenth and sixteenth centuries, and to appraise Venice's gradual involvement in the Renaissance, we must first look to the political background, to the political factors that led the Republic to embark on the conquest of the mainland area around the Lagoon. This move was dictated by the necessity of creating a "buffer state" between Venice herself and the hostile city states of Northern Italy. To do so, she required a land army of her own to protect the city and to impose her will on the mainland governments; for its levying and maintenance such an army required the supporting organization of a modern state on a broad territorial basis. Such was the process involved, and as she pursued it Venice saw that Florence had taken the lead in the new Renaissance culture; she accordingly followed that lead, set herself to absorb all that was most vital in the new art, and prepared to take the lead herself.

Her triumph came in the time of Titian, which opens the fourth period of Venetian history. That period began with the war against the League of Cambrai or, more exactly, with the decisions taken at the Peace of Bologna (1529-1530). For the situation in the opening decade of the sixteenth century was again very much what it was at the time of the war of Chioggia: the European powers had formed a coalition against Venice and were bent on her destruction.

After her defeat at the battle of Agnadello (1509), Venice lay defenceless before the converging armies of the Pope, the Emperor and the King of France. For a time she thought herself doomed, but circumstances combined to save her *in extremis*, through no merit of her own. Yet one undoubted merit she did have: that of undertaking and carrying through the necessary reorganization of her political life. She was wise enough, in the opening phase of this fourth period, to call a halt to her policy of building up a land empire, wise enough to redirect her energies into administrative reform and self-preservation. She saw that her interest lay in peace and diplomacy, not in reckless ambitions and exhausting wars. The political map of Europe had changed and Venice, if she was to survive, had to adapt herself to new conditions of life.

She accordingly set herself to make the most of every asset: the bureaucratic apparatus of administration was made more efficient, agricultural production was increased, and in a short time Venice became a thriving industrial power. In the early years of the sixteenth century she sought to enlist the support of the Sultan of Turkey for a project of putting a canal through the isthmus of Suez—the only effective means, as she saw, of competing with the Portuguese who had opened up the ocean trade routes. But the project came to nothing, for it belonged in effect to the old policy of adventure and expansion which had now been superseded. The Venetians preferred, no doubt rightly, to invest their wealth at home in the city and the mainland provinces; rightly, for it was this exploitation of her home resources, and the resulting reorganization of her national economy, that enabled Venice to survive for another three centuries.

Now that she had renounced her aggressive policies and her dreams of power and empire, the myth of Venice took shape in men's minds, awed as they were by the efficiency of her government and dazzled by the splendour and luxury of Venetian life—a myth that took on extraordinary proportions in the eighteenth century, and is still alive today. For the fifth period distinguishable in the history of Venice is that through which the city is living now. Present-day Venice, as a Baroque author might put it, lives on serenely in her ivory tower, receiving the homage of countless visitors and enjoying the fruits of her past.

★

Despite her many-sided history, despite the multiplicity of influences and styles and cultural strata, despite the often puzzling survivals and contradictions which, in the foregoing pages, we have sought to trace to their basic elements and determining forces, the fact remains that each phase of Venetian history and each work of Venetian art is unmistakably distinctive of Venice herself, so characteristic indeed as to stand conspicuously apart from that of any other civilization. To give so peculiarly Venetian a character to her art and her way of life, to a city as multiform and effervescent as a bazaar, to give unity to so many constituent elements, so various in their origin— to do that required the shaping and steadying action of certain constant factors of race and environment which, we shall find, are always present and operative in every-thing Venetian. Each century, each style, each object, each person, acted on by those factors, acquired the luminous and indelible citizenship of its small island home.

Of primordial importance is the uniqueness of the site. Anyone who has lived in a country traversed by waterways, on the shores of a lake or the sea, knows what it means to be continuously surrounded by the restless murmuring of water and the gleams that play on its surface. "The spirit of the waters," writes Horatio F. Brown, "free, vigorous, and pungent, had passed... into the being of the men who dwelt upon them. Venice, in this union of the people and the place, declared the nature of her personality, a personality so infinitely various, so rich, so pliant..."

"Water," as Goethe writes, "was at once street, square and promenade. The Venetian was forced to become a new creature; and Venice can only be compared with itself." Man, in the barren islands of the Lagoon, must fend for himself, and there his needs have always been the measure of all things: Venice was made in his image, to such an extent that not even Modern Times and Modern Progress have appreciably altered it. The lagoon dweller is not a man who is much inclined to metaphysical abstractions. Of necessity a seafarer, living close to nature, compelled to adjust each day's occupa-tions to water, wind and weather, he was practical-minded in his attitude to things and his dealings with people. He appreciated the good things of life, clinging to and making the most of every asset past and present. This practical turn of mind, this close, almost loving contact with the material side of life, goes far to account for two other fundamental strains in the Venetian make-up: the respect for the past and the extroverted character of the whole city.

The merchant, by instinct, avoids set plans of action and preconceived ideas: his way is to capitalize on unforeseen circumstances whenever they arise. He neither disowns the past nor sets up the present against it. It is this open-mindedness that accounts for the persistence of old traditions in Venice and, at the same time, the general willingness to accept new ideas. Her history is one of continuous growth. Just as no law of long standing and tried effectiveness was ever revoked, so no monument was pulled down or work of art replaced merely because it belonged to the past.

Venice was the home of a human society where men of all races, colours and creeds rubbed shoulders, where strange and unexpected encounters were to be made. And indeed, as Berengo has recently written, "Venice retains even today the physiognomy of a city that stood on the frontier between Europeans and Turks, Armenians and Greeks, Catholics and Protestants, Orthodox Jews and Moslems."

According to legend Venice came into existence on the 25th of March, A.D. 421. On the 12th of May, 1797, the government fell and the Republic was at an end. An unbroken succession of one hundred and twenty Doges ruled Venice for over a thousand years, giving her stable government and, for much of that time, the power to forward great ambitions. The marvel is that from beginning to end a few slips of land in a desolate lagoon should have sheltered such a State; that its leaders should have sprung again and again from the same great families (Mocenigo, Grimani, Contarini, Corner, etc.); that in all that time the city should never have been a prey to revolution or seriously disturbed by factions, but steadily abided by the spirit and the laws that had served it so well in the past. This continuity justifies us in comparing and correlating different periods of Venetian history which, in their correspondences and contrasts, are likely to throw light on each other.

As early as 1009, for example, we hear of the inspection, by officials representing the Doge Ottone Orseolo, of goods intended for export. The practice was sanctioned by law, and down to the end of the Republic an office of government inspectors was responsible for maintaining the professional standards of the trade guilds and the high quality of Venetian products. Such vigilance may in part explain why the history of Venetian art is unmarked by the crises and breaks of continuity that chequer the art history of other cities. The unvarying excellence of Venetian colours and paper, of Venetian wool and silk, of Venetian workmanship in general, served to create standards of quality which were never suffered to decline and which undoubtedly took effect in the field of art.

If there is a city in the world whose soul is transparently mirrored in its arts, that city is Venice. The Venetian has a knack of revealing himself, of conveying the one aspect of his personality best calculated to cast its spell over others. And the charm of the whole city springs from this individual charm, multiplied many times over, just as the beauty of Venetian architecture is compounded of the blithe and buoyant charm of each individual façade. Overt, unreserved, self-revealing—here we have another fundamental characteristic of the city.

By the time Venice assumed her mature physiognomy under Doge Sebastiano Ziani in the latter half of the twelfth century, she was truly an open city, alone of medieval towns in having neither walls nor gates, neither towers nor drawbridges. Hers was an ideal style of architecture, made for peace, not for war.

THE WINGED LION OF ST MARK, ON THE COLUMN IN THE PIAZZETTA.
PERSIAN ART OF THE SASSANIAN PERIOD (FOURTH CENTURY A.D.).

The encroaching waters leave but little space in which to build; hence the constant effort to build well and lastingly. The doors of the armoury, for example, in the Ducal Palace, were not made of ordinary timber, but of cedar of Lebanon, a sweet-smelling wood, and one not liable to decay, obtained in the East at great expense through the Venetian consul at Aleppo. The great slabs of the marble pavement in St Mark's and the enormous columns in the Piazzetta commanded the respect of all who saw them, as testifying to the feats of enterprise accomplished by Venetian ships in bringing them all the way from the East. Every monument and painting, in every part of Venice, bore witness to a passion for beautifying the city, for multiplying and displaying its wealth.

Doge Pietro Orseolo (976-978), by his will, set aside part of his personal fortune for the purpose of increasing the magnificence of Palace ceremonies and public rejoicings. St Mark's Square became, as it were, the stage of a grandiose theatre, where the arrival of the new Doge and his induction into office were celebrated with fitting pomp and ceremony. For the Venetians loved the theatre and theatrical display in all its forms, and indeed all in Venice offered a pretext for showmanship and pageantry. Only the mood changes: now solemn and pompous, now frivolous and freakish, now noisy and commonplace.

Painting is the representative art of Venice. Introduced—according to Sansovino—earlier than any of the other arts, it conveys, inimitably, century after century, the colourful, extroverted character of the city. Titian, for example, always kept his eye on the world around him, eager to fathom and exalt life in all its forms. His genius was untrammelled by intellectual preconceptions and metaphysical systems. What he learned from the Tuscan Renaissance had nothing to do with formal values or abstract rules. He learned to share what was undoubtedly the fundamental creed of Florentine civilization: the exaltation of man as the vital centre of the world, man immersed in nature, which nourishes him and recognizes his sovereignty.

Venice, an open city both in her urban structure and in her spiritual outlook, retains that characteristic even today. All that was once alive in her history is now quiescent, but she has accepted her new life and made the best of it: no more wars and conquests, no more bold sea ventures, no more stately ceremonies and inspired creations of the mind, but the admiring homage paid by men of all nations to her art treasures and the monuments and lessons of her past.

This bronze lion was brought from the East and placed on top of one of the two columns in the Piazzetta, where it became the symbol of St Mark. (The other column has a statue of St Theodore, the original patron saint of Venice.) The lion, like the bronze horses on the façade of St Mark's, was taken down by the French in 1797 and sent to Paris; it was returned to Venice in 1815.

BYZANTINE ICON WITH THE ARCHANGEL MICHAEL, HALF-LENGTH. REPOUSSÉ RELIEF IN GOLD, WITH ENAMELS.
TENTH OR ELEVENTH CENTURY. TREASURE OF ST MARK'S.

2

THE BYZANTINE HERITAGE

Venice arose in the shadow of imperial Byzantium. In the formative period of her history, and for centuries thereafter, Venice looked to the East and was receptive to the influence of Byzantine art. More products, and finer ones, of the workshops of Constantinople can be seen in Venice today than anywhere else in the world, and in visiting her palaces, churches and museums one comes to realize that Venetian art itself in its earlier phases was an offshoot of Byzantine art. Throughout the Middle Ages Venice lay within the sphere of influence of that art, at a time when its productive energies were at their height, and the outstanding creation of Venetian art, the church of St Mark's, is the very symbol and embodiment of the Venetian debt to Byzantium.

This is not the place for an extended account of the political and economic relations between Byzantium and Venice; suffice it to say that those relations were instrumental in bringing about the penetration of Byzantine art into the great merchant city of the Adriatic. It is essential, however, to give a chronological outline of the historical circumstances affecting the influx of Byzantine works of art and Byzantine tastes into Venice. This period begins in the ninth century and extends to the last third of the thirteenth century; from the time, that is, of the great rivalry between the Empire of the East and the Empire of the West, under Charlemagne and his successors, down to the short-lived Latin Empire of Constantinople (1204-1261), largely founded and supported by the Venetians themselves. In the ninth century, opposed as they were to the encroachments of the Carolingian Empire, which had extended its hegemony to the northern shores of the Adriatic, the Venetians turned for support to the Emperor of the East and proclaimed their fidelity to him.

Venice remained outside the Carolingian Empire by submitting to the overlordship of Byzantium, which on the whole treated its vassal leniently and—most important of all—enabled it gradually to enrich itself by trading with the Mediterranean lands dependent on Constantinople. The economic advantages that accrued to Venice from its friendship with Byzantium increased with the passage of time, particularly from the end of the eleventh century on. By then the Venetians had secured from Byzantium substantial and far-reaching economic privileges which enabled them in the twelfth century, under the Comnene dynasty, to exert a very considerable political influence within the Byzantine Empire. Increasing competition on the part of the other merchant cities of Italy, Genoa and Pisa, failed to check the growing power of the Venetian State, which reached its height following the sack of Constantinople by the Crusaders in 1204, when the Latin Empire of the East was founded on the shores of the Bosporus. It was during the next half-century, until the fall of the Latin Empire in 1261, that the Venetians reaped the greatest commercial advantages from their connections with the Byzantine East.

The period that followed was not so brilliant, but until the fall of Constantinople in 1453 the Venetians maintained the closest contacts with the remnants of the Empire of the East and its heirs. To Venice herself in fact fell a large share of that heritage, in Crete and elsewhere, and long after the Ottoman Turks had established themselves at Constantinople Venice remained a presence to be reckoned with in the lands of Byzantine tradition.

This later period forms a kind of aftermath to the history of the great age in the relations between Venice and Byzantium, and this aftermath too found its particular expression in the arts of Venice. We shall have something to say about it at the end of this chapter, which however will be mainly devoted to the Byzantine contribution to Venetian art during the earlier period. It was then that Byzantine influence was brought to bear most steadily and tellingly on the largest number of works, including those whose quality makes them of the highest interest to us here. For Venice was fortunate in apprenticing herself to the Byzantine masters at the very time of their finest achievements.

The great memorial, indeed the living symbol, of the close relations between Byzantium and Venice is St Mark's, originally the chapel of the Palace of the Doges, which became the central edifice of the city. St Mark's is a highly complex structure almost miraculously combining elements of different periods and origins in perfect harmony. Here we find a combination typical of the artistic relations between Byzantium and Venice: basic elements purely Byzantine in character, interpreted and added to in a purely Venetian manner. Typical again is the Venetian way of elaborating wholly Byzantine forms: nowhere else in Western Europe do we find so ready and faithful an imitation of Byzantine originals, in all techniques, from masonry to enamels. Lastly, St Mark's testifies to another peculiarity of the relations between Byzantium and Venice: the extraordinary length of time over which Venice remained open to Byzantine influence. What was roughed out in the ninth century was worked over in

WEST FAÇADE OF THE CHURCH OF ST MARK'S. BYZANTINE ARCHITECTURE. FINISHED IN THE LATE ELEVENTH CENTURY.

the eleventh, completed in the thirteenth and renewed in the fourteenth. Here again Venice was alone in thus maintaining contact with Byzantium over a period of centuries, not only receptive to its works of art but welcoming them, whether earlier or contemporary works. This is proof enough of constant intercourse and familiarity with the things and people of the Byzantine East. What elsewhere was an episode or an interlude was in Venice the rule for long centuries. It is important to realize what this meant in the domain of the arts because of its bearing on a major event in the history of the Church. For, curiously enough, by far the greater part of this enrichment of Venice through the influence of Byzantine art dates from after the schism of 1054. In other words, it was effectively brought about, generation after generation, despite the separation of the Greek from the Roman Church. The power and appeal of art, even religious art, was such as to overshadow the quarrel between ecclesiastics.

VIEW OF THE INTERIOR OF ST MARK'S, LOOKING TOWARDS THE ALTAR.

VIEW OF THE DOMES OF ST MARK'S.

The raised sanctuary of the church, shown on the opposite page, is divided from the nave by an iconostasis of polychrome marble, composed of eight columns supporting a heavy architrave with marble statues of the Virgin, St John the Baptist and the Apostles. One of the masterpieces of Venetian Gothic sculpture, it is the work of the brothers Jacobello and Pier Paolo Dalle Masegne and dates to 1394. Beyond the iconostasis is the high altar with the famous Pala d'Oro. The apse mosaic represents Christ enthroned. In the central cupola at the top is the Ascension mosaic. Only the standing figures of the Virgin, two angels and several Apostles are visible in our photograph. Between the windows are figures personifying the Christian virtues; beneath them, on the pendentives, are two Evangelists shown writing their Gospels. The view of the eleventh-century domes (above), each topped by a small lantern tower, shows clearly the cruciform plan of the church.

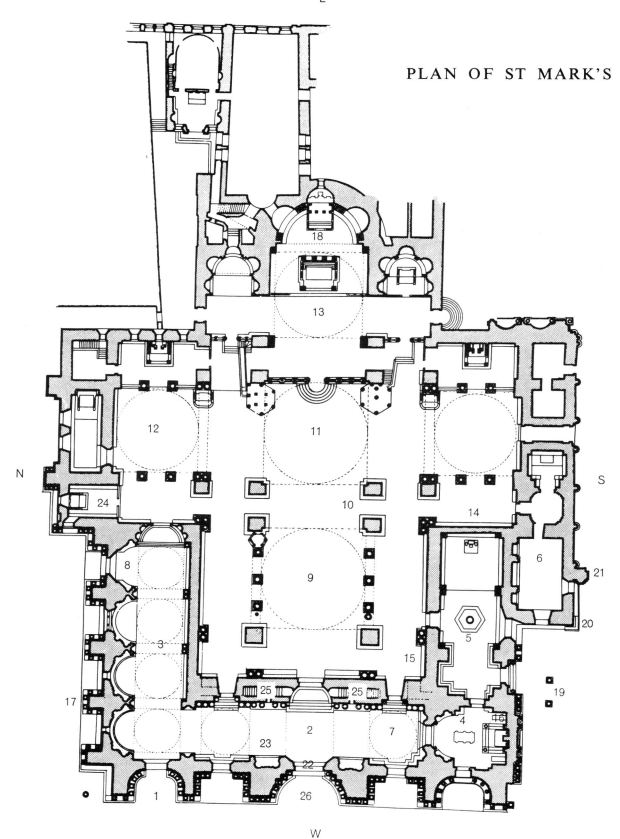

PLAN OF ST MARK'S

E

N

S

W

1 Porta Sant'Alipio
2 West Atrium
3 North Atrium
4 Zeno Chapel
5 Baptistery Chapel
6 Treasure
7 Creation Mosaic
8 Exodus Mosaic
9 Dome of the Pentecost
10 Crucifixion Mosaic

11 Dome of the Ascension
12 Dome of St John the Evangelist
13 Dome of Christ-Emmanuel
14 Mosaic of the Discovery of the
   Relics of St Mark
15 Deesis
16 Virgin and Child
   (Aniketos)
17 Ascension of Alexander
18 Pala d'Oro

19 Pillars of Acre
20 Four Tetrarchs
21 Porta della Carta
   (main entrance of Ducal Palace)
22 Bronze Horses (on the Loggia dei Cavalli)
23 Tomb of Dogesse Felicita Michiel
24 Cappella dei Mascoli
25 Stairways leading to Museo di San Marco
   and Loggia dei Cavalli
26 Main Entrance

St Mark's as we see it today in the Piazza of Venice is not the first religious edifice to occupy that site and serve as the chapel of the neighbouring palace of the Doges (i.e., the Dukes) of Venice. It would seem, moreover, that the original oratory erected there was dedicated to another saint, one even more closely connected with Byzantium than St Mark, the soldier martyr Theodore. The dedication of the palace chapel was changed when the body of St Mark the Evangelist, stolen from a church at Alexandria by some Venetian merchants, was brought to Venice in the year 828. Now a reliquary chapel, like so many other "holy chapels" in Western Europe, St Mark's was rebuilt on the cruciform plan of other churches dedicated to the Apostles, and modelled more particularly on the famous church of the Holy Apostles in Constantinople, which for centuries had housed the relics of three Apostles. The ninth-century church of St Mark's was again entirely rebuilt in the second half of the eleventh century (consecrated in 1071); the cruciform plan was maintained and again, for the second time, as a roughly contemporary chronicle expressly tells us, the edifice was designed in imitation of the church of the Holy Apostles in Constantinople. The main structure of St Mark's as we see it today dates from this period. It is a vast cruciform edifice crowned with five domes: one dome over each arm of the cross, together with a central dome. From inside the church these hemispherical cupolas, though covered with mosaics, are clearly visible; outside, however, the original silhouette is concealed by roofs added in the thirteenth century which have nothing Byzantine about them. The domes are supported by huge pillars connected by arches, in accordance with a Byzantine system of architecture, the original model—the church of the Holy Apostles in Constantinople—having been adhered to as regards all the essential features of the construction.

Take for example the four pillars of the central dome, which are divided into four elements by narrow passages: this structural unit has its model in the Justinian architecture of Constantinople, its original source undoubtedly being the church of the Holy Apostles. For it is definitely the architecture of the sixth century that was so assiduously imitated at Venice in the ninth, then again in the eleventh and even in the thirteenth century. In other words, the peculiarly Byzantine features of St Mark's, which were to give direction and impetus to all Venetian architecture in the Middle Ages, have their origin in the monumental art of Late Antiquity as exemplified at Constantinople. From this art derives the conception of space in the interior of St Mark's—space created by semicircular arches and hemispherical domes resting on columns and walls veneered with polychrome marbles. This space is unevenly lighted, growing brightest at the foot of the domes that rise over the naves, then gradually dimmer as we move into the side aisles. This play of light and shade, or rather of pools of shadow around a nucleus of light, already very marked in St Sophia at Constantinople, was much more distinct in St Mark's in its original state, when galleries occupying the whole width of the aisles ran round the interior of the church. It was because of the darkness of these side aisles beneath the galleries that in the twelfth century the original galleries were replaced by the rather curious "catwalks" now to be found above the colonnades of the naves. On the whole, the interior of St Mark's is a Venetian version of the church of the Holy Apostles in Constantinople—which is not to say that St Mark's does not depart from its prototype in some secondary but often conspicuous respects (e.g., the apses, the crypt, the side chapels).

The eleventh-century church extended as far as the present main (i.e., west) façade, the original cruciform building having included a transversal vestibule. There is much less certainty as to the date of the north and south wings of the vestibule (the south wing is now a baptistery chapel). They may have been added after 1100, very likely in the thirteenth century. But even so, this type of vestibule or atrium surrounding the nave on three sides answers to a structural formula common in Byzantine architecture. So that in modifying the church originally modelled on the Holy Apostles the Venetians of this period nevertheless kept to the current practices of Byzantine architecture. And they did so again when, over this tripartite atrium (consisting of a single storey), they added a kind of terrace or outside gallery, which still exists in part. Though ignorant of their structural details, we know that terraces of this kind were frequently built in front of and around the churches of Constantinople and other Byzantine cities in the Middle Ages. Finally, in the thirteenth century, when the terraces of St Mark's were built, the façade was also enriched with a sumptuous architectural décor. With its five doorways standing in deep niches alternately rounded and rectilinear, its clustered columns receding one behind the other, and its semicircular arches, this façade seems to have been inspired by the architectural décor of walls of the type of the *scenae frontes* or by an antique triumphal arch. What we have here may indeed be a deliberate imitation of the triumphal monuments of Late Antiquity. Such is known to have been the case not only for the façades of certain Syrian churches of the sixth century (Resafa), but also for several Romanesque churches of the eleventh and twelfth centuries (Lincoln, Saint-Denis, Saint-Gilles). The assumption is all the more plausible at St Mark's in view of the fact that the new façade was crowned by a group of four bronze horses brought from Constantinople; for this quadriga here occupies the position normally assigned to it on triumphal arches. A mosaic of the period, in St Mark's itself (on the tympanum over the Sant'Alipio doorway), represents the church with this façade, and the care with which the four horses are represented on it (in the manner traditionally reserved since Antiquity for the representation of quadrigae) leaves no doubt as to the intentions of those responsible for this arrangement. The idea of a triumph is again suggested by the choice of reliefs let into the façade, above the niches formed by the doorways: two reliefs with Hercules and two others representing warrior saints, an archangel and the Virgin patroness (in prayer).

Originally the doorposts of the castle of San Saba at Acre, on the Palestine coast, the two Pillars of Acre (only one of them is shown here) were brought to Venice in the thirteenth century and set up in the square on the south side of St Mark's. The porphyry group of four Tetrarchs, represented as two pairs of warriors in armour embracing each other, is probably a trophy brought from Byzantium in the thirteenth century; the walls against which they are placed are those of the Treasure of St Mark's. Visible on the far right is part of the Porta della Carta, main entrance of the Ducal Palace.

ONE OF THE PILLARS OF ACRE (LEFT) AND THE PORPHYRY GROUP OF FOUR TETRARCHS (RIGHT).
SOUTH SIDE OF ST MARK'S, NEAR THE PORTA DELLA CARTA (FAR RIGHT).

This manner of historiating the façade of St Mark's has no parallel in any known monument of Constantinople. But indirect evidence (which cannot be set forth here) suggests that there were in fact Byzantine precedents for this practice. Constantinopolitan art of the eleventh and twelfth centuries, centring on the imperial palace, might have given us some information about these supposed models, but little or nothing now remains of that court art. Russian residences of this period, however, which were also inspired by Byzantine architecture, provide a number of clues. As for the architectural expression of the new façade of St Mark's (the same façade we see there today), the two superimposed orders of columns bring to mind the imitation of a two-storied portico, such as could still be seen in Constantinople in the sixth century; perhaps indeed it imitates the portico of the church of the Holy Apostles itself, this portico, adjacent to the atrium of the Holy Apostles, being adapted in Venice to the function of a façade. It was just at this time, moreover, in the thirteenth century, that the square in front of St Mark's was paved with flagstones; later the square was surrounded by stately buildings with columns and arcades which still today convey the impression of a vast atrium.

The incomparably rich and even sumptuous effect produced by the façade of St Mark's is due not only to its profusion of marble columns but also to the incrustations of polychrome slabs of stone—a practice that was to be generally adopted for the decoration of Venetian façades, both of churches and palaces. Today no such incrustations are any longer to be found in Constantinople, so that they may seem to be a Venetian invention. But the façades of the great Justinian churches were already inlaid with these plaques of polished marble; the Venetians, therefore, merely followed a Byzantine example, thus taking inspiration in still another respect from the ancient monuments of the Eastern capital, of which, unfortunately, so little has come down to us.

On the other hand, the practice of inlaying the walls of buildings with reliefs of various sizes, some figurative, some ornamental, originated in the *medieval* art of Byzantium. It was taken over by the Venetians, in St Mark's to begin with, and subsequently in the façades of other churches and palaces, where large numbers of such reliefs were employed. The oldest of them, and a good many others of different periods, were brought to Venice from the Byzantine East. Such is the case, for example, on the façade of St Mark's, of the relief of Hercules with a boar and another representing St Demetrius. The curious relief on the north façade, representing the Ascension of Alexander, is again a Byzantine original. Several of the reliefs on religious subjects inside the church also come from Byzantium. Some of these, in particular, are works of art of a very high order, notably the monumental relief in the south aisle representing the Deesis and several reliefs of the Virgin, for example the Virgin and Child called Aniketos ("The Invincible") in a Greek inscription and at least two Virgins in the Orant position (i.e., lifting their arms in prayer). One of these, the so-called Madonna della Grazia, numbers among the finest achievements in the antique style of eleventh

DEESIS: CHRIST BETWEEN THE VIRGIN AND ST JOHN THE BAPTIST. BYZANTINE RELIEFS.
PROBABLY LATE TENTH OR ELEVENTH CENTURY. SOUTH AISLE OF ST MARK'S.

century Byzantine sculpture. As always in Venice, the local craftsmen lost no time
in imitating the Byzantine carvings imported from the East. In St Mark's, elsewhere in
Venice and throughout the surrounding region, we find these local imitations, varying a
good deal in quality, but keeping on the whole to a fairly high standard; they represent
for the most part saints and Biblical figures in a monumental style, or birds and
confronted animals, in a setting carved in relief. All these carvings tend to imitate
Byzantine originals, being distinguished from them in various degrees by realistic
features added, perhaps involuntarily, by the Venetian imitators. There must have
been a steady demand for them over a period of time, for they were produced in far
greater numbers than in the Greek workshops that specialized in similar carvings.
There was, likewise, an abundant production of goldsmiths' work and imitation enamels in Venice in the thirteenth century, with the result that the market was flooded

VIRGIN AND CHILD ENTHRONED, CALLED "ANIKETOS" (THE INVINCIBLE). BYZANTINE RELIEF.
PROBABLY THIRTEENTH CENTURY. CAPPELLA ZENO, ST MARK'S.

THE ASCENSION OF ALEXANDER THE GREAT, BORNE UP BY TWO GRIFFINS. BYZANTINE RELIEF.
NORTH FAÇADE OF ST MARK'S.

with them, completely ousting similar Byzantine products. Venetian craftsmen, appreciating their value and rarity, were among the first to study and familiarize themselves with Byzantine works of art; grasping the commercial possibilities of that art, they applied themselves to producing less costly versions of all such works as had been imported from Byzantium.

This is equally true of an art form that had long been the particular glory of Byzantium: mosaics. The Venetians were among the first in the West to appreciate at its true value the art of the medieval Byzantine mosaic. Having imported Greek mosaics into Venice, they called in Byzantine artists to produce similar works in Venice itself. The interior of St Mark's owes its splendour to the gorgeous mosaics of the domes and vaults.

Certain parts of this decoration are the work of Greek mosaicists, others were executed by their Venetian disciples, still others by Venetians who, without losing contact with their Byzantine models, interpreted them more freely, on lines of their own; and it was these local artists who are responsible for most of the mosaics in St Mark's and for many others in and around Venice, at Murano and Torcello. Even today, as many a tourist has seen for himself, the traditional technique of mosaic work is still practised by Venetian craftsmen.

We have no way of knowing when the art of the mosaic was first introduced into Venice. It cannot be said for certain whether the ninth-century church of St Mark's was decorated with Byzantine mosaics, though this may well have been the case. In Byzantium itself the long period of Iconoclasm, which had greatly restricted the activities of the mosaic workshops, did not come to an end until 843; even then it must have taken some time to train a new generation of technicians. But in the church of St Mark's as rebuilt late in the eleventh century we may take it for granted that the interior decorations included mosaics. Indeed, the consensus of opinion today is that, in the main, the oldest mosaics in the present church either date from this period or follow fairly closely the iconographic programme laid down for the decoration of the new church towards the end of the eleventh century. Some students of the question go even further and, in view of the close architectural relationship between St Mark's and the church of the Holy Apostles in Constantinople, they feel that the mosaics in the former probably imitated those in the latter. But it is well not to give too much weight to this hypothesis, considering the great distance in time that separated the monumental images in the Holy Apostles (whether executed in the sixth or in the ninth century) and the mosaics placed on the vaults of St Mark's which, after all, were not built until the late eleventh century. The art of the two churches could scarcely have been the same. The most one can reasonably conjecture is that the Venetians may have taken over certain subjects of the mosaic cycle in the Holy Apostles and, as regards the position and arrangement of them on the walls and vaults, may have followed the example they found ready to hand in the great church of the Byzantine capital. The mosaics in the Holy Apostles (and the church itself) having been destroyed by the Turks in the fifteenth century, all we have to go on are the descriptions of them given by Byzantine writers. Meagre though they are, these descriptions make it clear that only a single important image in St Mark's—the Descent of the Holy Spirit (Pentecost) in the west dome of the nave—corresponds in subject and position to a mosaic in the Holy Apostles. True, the scenes of martyrdom of the different Apostles in the side aisles of the nave of St Mark's repeat a cycle that also figured in the church of the Holy Apostles. But for the rest, as far as we can tell, the mosaics in St Mark's follow those in the Holy Apostles neither in their subject matter nor in their arrangement. The two groups of mosaics have, needless to say, a few points in common, but hardly more than is to be expected in works based in each case on the stock themes of Christian iconography.

There can be no doubt, however, that the mosaicists employed in St Mark's often drew inspiration from the Byzantine works of their time, and a number of parallels can easily be established with mosaics and wall paintings of the eleventh and twelfth centuries in Byzantine and para-Byzantine lands. Certain aspects of the St Mark mosaics are in this respect highly characteristic: the image of the Ascension figuring at the top and on the sides of a cupola (at St Mark's, in the central dome); the Gospel cycle on the vaults around the cupolas, the accent here being laid on episodes corresponding to the great liturgical feasts, with special emphasis on the Crucifixion and the Harrowing of Hell, for theological reasons (since these two themes refer to the death and resurrection of the Saviour). No less characteristic of the mosaic cycles in medieval Byzantine churches are the medallions, enclosing either half- or full-length saints, which occupy the spaces available on either side of the main scenes. Extensive series of such medallions are to be seen in St Mark's, both in the apse and on the arches and in the narrow passages between the great pillars, beneath the domes.

This is not to say that the mosaic ensemble in St Mark's consists merely of faithful imitations of Greek models; far from it. The fact is that many features of these mosaics testify to the vigorous originality of the local craftsmen, whose share in the work can be assumed to have been a large one, considering the length of time it took to complete the decorations. Begun about 1100, the mosaics in the apse, nave and transept were still unfinished a century later; the work in this part of the church is known to have been still in progress early in the thirteenth century. The mosaics in the atrium progressed at about the same rate; it required another century, or very nearly so, to complete those in the domes and the surrounding vaults, and in the north and west sides of the atrium. Work produced in such leisurely fashion can safely be assigned to local craftsmen; specialists called in from afar would have done their work without delay and returned to their homes.

In the nave, despite the delays attending the work, a single iconographic programme seems in the main to have been adhered to, the programme which, as mentioned above, St Mark's has in common with Byzantine churches of the eleventh and twelfth centuries: grandiose visions of God in the cupolas along the longitudinal axis, surrounded by Gospel scenes and portraits of saints. In the atrium, on the other hand, where all the mosaics illustrate Old Testament episodes (from Genesis and Exodus), this art can be seen to evolve very distinctly from one bay to the next; the stylistic interpretation of the scenes, if not the actual programme, bears the imprint of Constantinopolitan art in its successive phases, corresponding to successive generations of mosaicists.

The peculiar contribution of the Venetians themselves is more clearly apparent in the choice of certain subjects which, in the position in which we find them, have no parallel in Byzantium, whereas in one way or another this approach answers to a Western tradition. Thus, among the oldest mosaics, we find the figures of Christ enthroned and

THE SIX DAYS OF CREATION AND THE STORY OF ADAM AND EVE (GENESIS I–III). MOSAIC. THIRTEENTH CENTURY.
SOUTH CUPOLA OF THE WEST ATRIUM OF ST MARK'S.

the Apostles (including Mark, the patron saint of the church) in the apse, and the group of Christ and the Apostles overhead as we enter the nave. The style of these images is Byzantine, but their position is not; it corresponds, rather, to the practice obtaining in Latin churches. Similarly, several series of mosaics at the base of the cupolas in the nave are foreign to the Byzantine tradition: the personifications of Virtues (central cupola), the Evangelist symbols (east cupola), the Fathers of the Latin Church (north cupola), and so forth. In most of these cases the iconography too is inspired by works of the Latin West. And it is in the West that we must also look for the origins of the art tradition which, though mingled with Byzantine undertones, characterizes the cycles of hagiographical images in the apsidal chapels and the two arms of the transept. The highly interesting scenes of this cycle (illustrating the lives of St Mark, St John the Evangelist and St Clement) glow with great bare tracts of gold, in the Byzantine manner, but contain at the same time a patterning more abstract and many details more realistic than at Byzantium.

The handiwork of Venetian mosaicists is equally distinct in the Exodus sequence of the north atrium and in the exterior mosaic over the Porta Sant'Alipio (west façade). Both date from the 1270s, and the façade mosaic in particular, showing the church of St Mark's as it was at that time, breaks away from Byzantine formulas and gives a direct representation of reality as the artist saw it.

It would, however, be wrong to say that the Venetian mosaicists *gradually* drew apart from their Byzantine exemplars. For in the thirteenth century, in the mosaics in the atrium, they modelled themselves on the illustrations in an old Greek manuscript (cf. page 48); and in the fourteenth century, in the baptistery mosaics, they again kept to Byzantine models—but contemporary Byzantine models. It is true that many motifs and forms borrowed from the Quattrocento art of Northern Italy are also to be found here. But in the pendentives of the cupola the large figures of the Greek Fathers of the Church are replicas of purely Byzantine mosaics of the same period to which the baptistery mosaics belong. It is this that proves beyond a doubt the continuity of the Byzantine tradition in Venice, despite the many departures from Byzantine models which at all times their Venetian admirers had permitted themselves. In other words, from the eleventh to the fourteenth century the Venetians showed themselves to be not only singularly receptive to the attractions of monumental Byzantine mosaic work, but also quite capable of interpreting Byzantine models on lines of their own.

Confronted by the large number of mosaics in St Mark's, the reader may find it helpful to have before him a summary of the main subjects, listed according to their position in the church. An exhaustive enumeration of the mosaics will be found in the standard work by Otto Demus (see Bibliography). What follows will suffice to bring home the point we here wish to make clear, namely, the extent to which the mosaic decorations in St Mark's were shaped by Byzantine influence.

West Façade. Only a single mosaic now remains (Porta Sant'Alipio), representing the transfer of the relics of St Mark the Evangelist to his Venetian church. This mosaic, a work of the thirteenth century, originally formed part of a sequence which included three other scenes from the story of the relics of St Mark, together with a Last Judgment and four Gospel scenes (in the tympana of the doors and above, on the façade).

West and North Sides of the Atrium. An unbroken cycle of mosaics, beginning with the Creation, ends with Moses leading the children of Israel through the wilderness. These were executed by successive teams of mosaicists from about 1210 to 1290, beginning with those in the south cupola of the west atrium and ending with those in the easternmost cupola of the north atrium. These mosaics, both in choice of subject matter and iconography, follow the illustrations in a Greek manuscript of the Bible now preserved in the British Museum (Cotton Bible, sixth century, possibly illuminated in Alexandria). Remarkable in the Exodus scenes (page 50) is the realism of the details: the quails that "at even came up and covered the camp" (note the woman roasting some at the far left) and Moses praying under the starry night-sky. In the Creation scenes (page 46) in the first cupola it is interesting to note the winged beings beside the Creator. On the first day there is only one of these "angels," on the second day there are two, on the third day three and so forth. Here we have a reflection of Plato's ideas as seen through the patristic writings of the early Church: each of these "angels" is the light in which is reflected the idea of all the creatures due to appear during the day (this explanation we owe to Mademoiselle d'Aherng). In the last bays of the atrium one is struck by the ease and skill with which these mosaicists of the late thirteenth century harked back, by way of their Early Christian models, to the style and idiom of antique art. At this period, both in Byzantium and in Italy (at Anagni, for example), artists were pursuing parallel lines of research based on similar antique models.

Nave and Aisles. Leaving aside the later mosaics and a host of secondary figures (chiefly portraits of saints), let us focus our attention on the mosaics on each cupola and the main figures accompanying them. These mosaics in the central part of the church must have been executed, in several successive phases, in the twelfth century.

The mosaic in the west dome of the nave, overhead as we enter the church, is the most markedly Byzantine of them all. It represents the Pentecost, with a throne made ready for the God-Judge *(Hetimasia)* at the top of the dome, surrounded by the twelve Apostles. Below them are the figures representing the various nations that witnessed the Descent of the Holy Spirit. Finally, on the pendentives are the archangels and, on the vaults of the side aisles, portraits of the Apostles and scenes of their martyrdom. The second dome, in the centre of the church, represents the Ascension, with the Christ Pantocrator, rising into the blue heaven, at the very top. Contrary to Byzantine practice, figures personifying the Christian Virtues occupy the walls of the dome

THE DESCENT OF THE HOLY SPIRIT ON THE APOSTLES (PENTECOST). MOSAIC. TWELFTH CENTURY.
WEST DOME OF THE NAVE OF ST MARK'S.

THE MIRACLE OF THE QUAILS AND MOSES BRINGING FORTH WATER FROM THE ROCK (EXODUS XVI-XVII). MOSAIC. THIRTEENTH CENTURY. NORTH ATRIUM OF ST MARK'S.

between the windows. Beneath them, on the pendentives, are the four Evangelists writing their Gospels (which is Byzantine) and images of the four rivers of Paradise (which is not). On the four arches supporting the dome is a sequence of Gospel scenes which, despite some surprising omissions, include the Childhood, Passion, Resurrection and Miracles of Christ. It is here, on the west arch, that the two most important scenes, from the dogmatic point of view, are brought together: the Crucifixion and the Resurrection of Christ (the Harrowing of Hell). At St Mark's as in all Byzantine churches of the Middle Ages they are placed in a conspicuous position. Both the iconography and the style of all these mosaics on Gospel themes are purely Byzantine. Their closest affinities are with Byzantine works of the twelfth century, although the design of the St Mark mosaics is more uneven and angular, and the movements of figures are noticeably more jerky than in the works of Greek artists.

The scenes in the north transept, illustrating the life of St John the Evangelist, are unique of their kind, though the scale of the figures is too small for the dome they occupy, their unskilled arrangement in space being even more evident in the corresponding dome of the south transept, where we find only four standing figures of saints. On the arches which from east to west flank these two domes are some complementary scenes of the Gospel cycle, in particular of Christ's Childhood. It is quite possible that these are later additions to the initial sequence.

The vaults over the choir are occupied by mosaics whose themes are in keeping with this part of the church. In the dome is a Christ-Emmanuel (i.e., the Logos as apart from the Incarnation) surrounded by the prophets and animals of Ezechiel's vision. This is a "cycle of heaven" displayed over the altar before reminding the faithful of the Incarnation and the intercession of God in favour of mankind (mosaics in the nave).

THE CRUCIFIXION. MOSAIC. THIRTEENTH CENTURY. WEST ARCH
OF THE CENTRAL DOME OF ST MARK'S.

As for the apse and the side chapels, St Mark the Evangelist is represented here, together with other saints whose relics were deposited in the church. Those responsible for this iconographic programme followed the practice generally prevailing in the West. As against this, Byzantine churches of the period had in the apse the figure of the Virgin with, above her, the Communion of the Apostles and the saints who wrote the Greek liturgy.

Chapels. The mosaics in the chapel of Sant'Isidoro, it is interesting to note (though they do not concern us here), are strongly imbued with Gothic influences from the West. Much superior works are the fourteenth-century mosaics in the Baptistery, with the curious angel figures in the cupola, the Fathers of the Greek Church on the pendentives and the cycle illustrating the life of St John the Baptist. One scene in this cycle is justly famous: Herod's Feast, with the graceful figure of Salome. The gorgeous solemnity of Byzantine work is here curiously blended with the mannered elegance of the so-called International Style of the European courts of the late fourteenth century.

If, as we have seen, the architecture and the mosaic decorations of St Mark's owe a very great deal to Byzantium, the debt to Byzantine art is no less great in the domain of the minor arts. In St Mark's itself, in the Treasure housed next door to the church, and in the Biblioteca Marciana on the Piazzetta, many are the pieces of church furniture and goldsmiths' work, glassware and enamels, embroideries and manuscripts illuminated and bound, that were brought to Venice from Constantinople and the Byzantine provinces. It is no exaggeration to say that nowhere else in the world can so fine a collection be found of these small masterpieces of flawless workmanship and taste which, for a period of centuries, the workshops of Constantinople alone were capable of producing. Those workshops and ateliers were, in the Early Middle Ages, virtually the only ones to maintain the art traditions of classical antiquity which, everywhere else in the civilized world, had been lost or temporarily eclipsed. Those who, in the West, were eventually to revive those traditions were in many cases initiated into them by the study of the sumptuary arts of Byzantium, and this is particularly true of the Venetians. In the Treasure of St Mark's and elsewhere in Venice we find many examples of a certain type of Venetian goldsmiths' work which, to begin with (in the thirteenth century), was an art industry of purely Byzantine inspiration. The Byzantine hall-mark is thus to be found, in the domain of portable art objects, first and foremost in a number of original works, some of them of exceptional value; and, secondly, in works of Venetian manufacture but of Byzantine inspiration which testify to the extraordinary prestige and influence of Byzantine art.

When Venice first gravitated into the political and economic system of the Eastern Emperor and became dependent on Constantinople, and later too, when her initiative and growing power earned her a privileged position within the Eastern Empire, the Byzantine emperors made periodic offerings and gifts to the churches of Venice. A small votive crown inset with fine enamels, now in the Treasure of St Mark's, may well have formed part of one of these imperial donations, the more so as it is adorned with a portrait of the Emperor of the East, Leo VI, the Wise (886-912). This emperor is known to have commissioned the building, at his own expense and perhaps by his own architects, of the church of San Zaccaria, just behind St Mark's, a few steps off the Riva degli Schiavoni. In St Mark's itself the great altarpiece of solid gold, known as the Pala d'Oro, a work unique in the world, contains the portrait of an Empress Irene, probably the wife of Alexis I Comnenus (1081-1118). This portrait, which must have been accompanied by one of her husband, undoubtedly comes from a piece of gold-smiths' work (not necessarily an altarpiece) presented to Venice by these Byzantine sovereigns. Many other costly objects, for both religious and secular use, must have been ordered by the Venetians themselves from Byzantine workshops or purchased in the East, by the Doges or their emissaries, and by Venetian merchants and travellers. Finally, in the early thirteenth century, Venice was enormously enriched by spoils from the churches and palaces of Constantinople after the sack of the Eastern capital by the Crusaders, at Venetian instigation, in 1204.

The Pala d'Oro stands today in all its splendour behind the high altar of St Mark's, and in the full glare of electric light its gold, enamels and precious stones glow and shimmer more brilliantly than they could ever have done in the Middle Ages. Its effect today chiefly depends on the gold and the polychrome ornaments lavishly added to it in the fourteenth century by Venetian goldsmiths trained in the school of Gothic decorative art. But the Pala is actually a far older work. Its present proportions and the arrange-ment of the many enamels on its surface date to the twelfth century. The enamels themselves, however, are of various origins, including two different series of them brought from Constantinople independently of each other. There are a good many small enamelled plaques at the top and on the frame which may well go back to the tenth century (and possibly to a previous Pala of 936). Seven large plaques at the top, six with Gospel scenes and one in the middle with an archangel, date from the twelfth century and come perhaps from the Monastery of the Pantocrator at Constan-tinople. The rest of the work was in all likelihood executed in Venice by Greek crafts-men and, very probably, their Venetian disciples. It must have taken them a good many years, being carried out in the eleventh or early twelfth century. This series of enamels includes all the figures in the central part of the Pala and the small scenes from the Gospel stories and the life of St Mark which surround them. In comparing these enamels one is tempted at first to distinguish between Greek work and local work and to assign different dates to them. But a more systematic examination should caution us against any such clear-cut distinction, for we find enamels whose style and technique show them to have in effect something of each of the two groups which, at first, seemed distinct both in date and place of origin, but which actually are not

The great altar screen known as the Pala d'Oro is the most splendid existing example of goldsmiths' and jewellers' work on a large scale. The seven enamel plaques on the top register represent the Archangel Michael (centre) and the six Feasts of the Church: the Entry into Jerusalem, the Harrowing of Hell, the Crucifixion, the Ascension, the Pentecost, and the Death of the Virgin. Below, in the centre, is Christ Blessing (Pantocrator), surrounded by the four Evangelists in medallions. Immediately above Christ is the Throne (Hetimasia) made ready for his coming. To either side are rows of angels, Apostles and Prophets. Beneath Christ are three panels with the figures of a Virgin Orant, the Empress Irene and Doge Ordelafo Falier. In addition to its 86 enamels, the Pala contains 1300 pearls, 400 garnets, 300 sapphires, 300 emeralds, 90 amethysts, 75 balas rubies, 15 rubies, 4 topazes and 2 cameos.

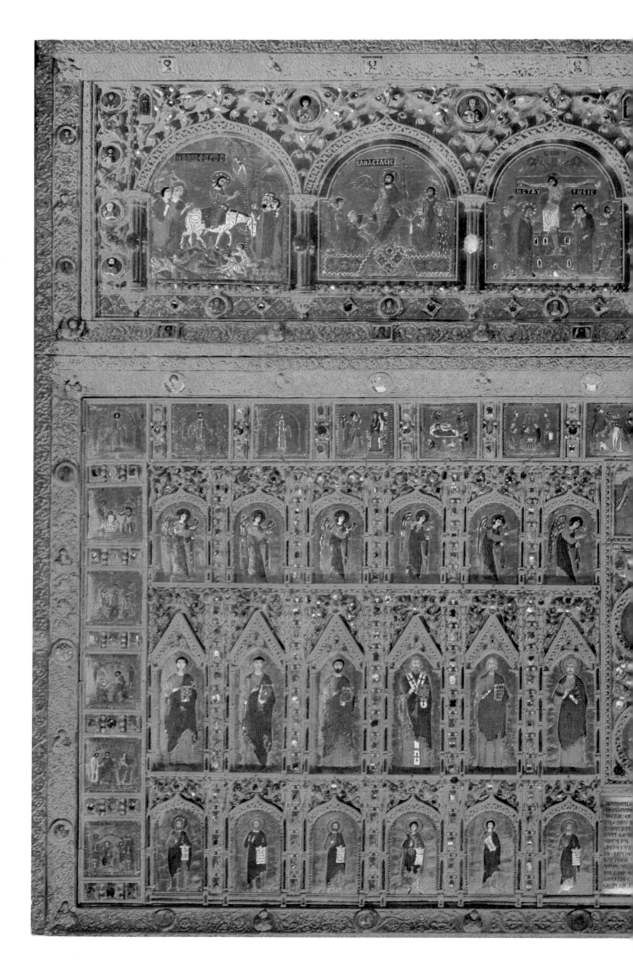

THE PALA D'ORO. GOLD ALTAR SCREEN
WITH ENAMELS AND PRECIOUS STONES.
TENTH TO FOURTEENTH CENTURY.
HIGH ALTAR OF ST MARK'S.

so very far apart. One is accordingly forced to conclude that, in spite of the peculiarities of style and colouring that distinguish them, and in spite of the fact that some are inscribed in Greek, some in Latin, all these enamels could well have been produced in the same workshops, but probably by different craftsmen and over a fairly long period of time. The Pala for which they were all originally made is presumably the one dated by subsequent chroniclers and inscriptions to 1105 and presented to the church by the Doge Ordelafo Falier; for his portrait figures on the lower register of the Pala, where it has clumsily been made to form a pendant to that of the Empress Irene, as a substitute for the missing portrait of her imperial husband. Contrary to what has often been stated, the portrait of Falier is not an emperor's portrait recast and converted into that of a Doge; the costume is not that of a Byzantine *basileus*, nor does the portrait form a symmetrical pendant to that of the Empress Irene, which is somewhat larger.

The choice and arrangement of the principal enamels on the Pala d'Oro answer to a particular purpose, the altarpiece having been originally conceived as an iconostasis on a reduced scale. Thus it is that on either side of the Christ Pantocrator and the

THE PALA D'ORO, DETAIL: THE BAPTISM OF CHRIST. CLOISONNÉ ENAMEL WITH PRECIOUS STONES. PROBABLY TWELFTH CENTURY CENTRAL REGISTER, SEVENTH SCENE FROM THE LEFT. HIGH ALTAR OF ST MARK'S.

Evangelists we see superimposed rows of worshipping figures: a row of angels, another of Apostles, another of Prophets. What we have here is a Deesis (i.e., "supplication") representing, as on the great iconostases of the Middle Ages, many holy figures interceding with Christ on behalf of mankind. As always on these iconostases, the leading events of the story of the Salvation are represented—events consecrated by the six great Feasts of the Church. Finally, on the frame on either side, are scenes from the life of St Mark, patron saint of the church. Altarpieces of this type were never used in Byzantine churches, so that functionally speaking there is nothing Byzantine about the Pala d'Oro. It is characteristic of the Venetians that in these circumstances they should apply to the Pala a Byzantine iconographic programme and, what is more, adorn it with enamels which, though sometimes markedly departing from it in their style, and though probably executed in Venice, belong to the Byzantine tradition.

The enamels of the Pala d'Oro, like all the Byzantine enamels to be found in Venice, are executed in the technique known as cloisonné enamelling. The paste of the variously coloured enamels is inserted in compartments separated by partitions *(cloisons)* made of very thin plates or fillets of gold set on edge and secured to the ground. The upper edge of these fillets is visible on the surface of the finished enamel, forming a fine network of lines which go to define the contours and separate parts (for example, facial features or drapery folds) of the enamelled figure. These fillets and the small foundation plaque to which they are soldered are always made of fine gold. The art of the enamellist consisted in heating his work to just the right temperature required to melt and fuse these thin metal partitions simultaneously with the coloured enamels. These were inserted between the fillets in the form of powder, to ensure that as they turned into a liquid paste and then gradually dried they should retain the desired colour and exactly fill the space reserved for them. For it was by no means the least difficult part of the work to see that the coloured pastes rose flush with the upper edge of the thin gold partitions prepared for them.

The best Byzantine enamels, produced by the workshops of Constantinople, are all distinguished by the painstaking care with which—probably by means of a final polishing—the partitions and the enamels between them are made to form an absolutely even surface. The purity of the colours and above all the clear semi-transparency of the enamel pastes imitating flesh tints, the chromatic harmonies of finely shaded tones and the unerring precision and finesse of design obtained by the thin gold partitions separating the colour surfaces, are all equally distinctive of the finest Byzantine enamels. Not that all the enamels manufactured at Constantinople were *ipso facto* superior to those produced elsewhere. Indeed, on the Pala d'Oro itself we find Constantinopolitan enamels of exquisite workmanship (the small medallions) side by side with others, also from Constantinople, which are quite undistinguished (the large Gospel scenes), in addition to a number of local Venetian enamels (scenes of the life of St Mark) which are excellent pieces of work.

The foregoing remarks on the Byzantine enamels of the Pala d'Oro hold good for all the enamels of Byzantine origin in Venice that call for mention here. Before dealing with these, however, it may be well to raise a few points, both technical and aesthetic, which will serve to guide us in determining the relative age of the works in question. In the ninth century, and even in the tenth (chiefly no doubt in the early years of the century), the enamelling covers the whole available surface area. The background extending around figures and objects, in particular, is entirely enamelled. Then, even before the middle of the tenth century, it became the practice to confine the enamelling to the subject represented, which was thus made to stand out against a gold background. The first technique was an imitation of paintings; the second, which was destined to prevail, took advantage and made the most of the close kinship of enamelling with goldsmiths' work. Here, as in so many other art forms, it took time for artists to realize the possibilities inherent in a new technique.

The most exquisite enamels of all, with beautifully shaded colours and gossamer-thin fillets, often widely spaced with sweeping curves, date from the tenth and the early eleventh century. In these works the fine gold lines of the fillets are often intended merely to stress a fold or a contour, without necessarily separating areas of different colours. Works presenting peculiar difficulties of execution were carried out in this technique; for example, enamels applied to curved or spherical surfaces (such as the two icons with the archangel Michael in the Treasure of St Mark's, discussed below). Later the network of lines formed by the fillets was tightened up and the design schematized, with the resulting emergence of long straight lines and sharp angles, whose effect is often emphasized by a repetition of the same motif. And since at the same time the fillets tended to grow thicker, the network of golden lines patterning the surface became increasingly conspicuous, to the detriment of the areas of colour which they were originally intended only to delimit and throw into relief. The heyday of the Byzantine enamel does not extend beyond the twelfth century. Enamels were still being manufactured in the thirteenth and fourteenth centuries, but of inferior quality and often with inferior materials, copper in place of gold and debased colouring matter precluding tonal shadings and effects of translucency. The champlevé technique now made its appearance alongside the traditional cloisonné, the small copper plaques admitting of a greater thickness than the gold grounds of the earlier enamels.

In dealing below with some of the characteristic examples of such works preserved in St Mark's and its Treasure, and in the Marcian Library, we need only refer the reader to the foregoing survey to enable him to appreciate for himself the characteristics of the different enamels. Before we leave the church itself, however, mention must be made, if only in passing, of two outstanding works in different techniques, both of which were much appreciated in medieval Italy: the eleventh-century bronze doors of the atrium, decorated with flowered crosses; and the embroideries on religious themes, including an altar frontal of 1210-1230 with its original dedication.

THE PALA D'ORO, DETAIL: THE ARCHANGEL MICHAEL. CLOISONNÉ ENAMEL WITH PRECIOUS STONES. TWELFTH CENTURY. CENTRAL PLAQUE OF THE UPPER REGISTER. HIGH ALTAR OF ST MARK'S.

The rooms now occupied by the Treasure of St Mark's number among the oldest surviving parts of the great church. The government of Venice, which here in the Middle Ages hoarded up its riches, saw to it that they were as safely housed, and as far out of harm's way, as massive walls and vaults could make them. Yet we read in the ancient chronicles of a fire that ravaged the Treasure in the thirteenth century, which even then contained priceless pieces of Byzantine goldwork. Some of the objects destroyed by fire on this occasion are listed and described. We know, too, that in the course of centuries, down to the Napoleonic era, the Republic for one reason or another had to part with some of the precious objects, of the most varied origin, hoarded up

"THE SEAT OF ST MARK." MARBLE RELIQUARY SHRINE WITH BYZANTINE RELIEFS. SIXTH CENTURY. TREASURE OF ST MARK'S.

in the church Treasure. But it was also enriched from time to time and many a loss was thus made good, so that the extent and variety of its collections as we see them today are astonishing.

The collections as a whole give us a graphic idea of what, between the ninth and the fourteenth century, Byzantium was capable of supplying to a wealthy neighbour eager to acquire both holy and devotional objects and precious works of art. Into the first category fall the many reliquaries of all shapes and sizes which the Venetians brought back or imported from Byzantium. For the most part these gold caskets and cases, carefully wrought and sometimes bearing votive inscriptions, cannot be described as works of art. The most interesting of them, historically speaking, is a reliquary of the Holy Cross presented by a Byzantine empress. Of particular interest, too, are several small reliquaries, tiny cross-shaped boxes which must have been worn as pectoral crosses on a chain round the neck. Another reliquary casket, of the type called Stauro-theques (for it once contained a fragment of the True Cross), has on its lid an enamel representing the Crucifixion. Though in its day undoubtedly a fine piece of work, its artistic value is now much diminished by its poor state of preservation—the more so in the Treasure of St Mark's, where it is overshadowed by so many impeccable examples of the same art.

But of all the objects of piety in the Treasure, pride of place must go to a large marble reliquary in the form of a chair, known as the "Sedia di San Marco," or Seat of St Mark. Sizable though it is, it is still too small to have served as an actual seat for anyone, and a hollow space contrived in the lower part of it shows its original purpose to have been that of a reliquary shrine. The Sedia, moreover, is a work of the sixth century, and we know that in the Christian churches of Late Antiquity the codex containing the Gospels was placed on a piece of furniture in the form of a throne, which stood at the back of the choir or the ambo. The Sedia is no less interesting as a work of art, with its all-over decoration of reliefs which, despite a certain stiffness, are by no means lacking in expressive power. Represented on it are the Lamb in the Garden of Paradise, the Evangelists and their symbols, the Cross surrounded by the Evangelists, and angels blowing trumpets (an allusion to the Second Coming). The "Seat of St Mark" must have been carved in one of the lands of the Eastern Mediterranean—where exactly it is now impossible to say. All the other Byzantine objects preserved in the Treasure are much smaller in size. They are portable objects, almost all of them works whose artistic value depends on the skilful handling of a difficult technique and the intrinsic beauty of costly materials.

We need not linger over a series of glass vases cut with very prominent reliefs repre-senting hunters and aquatic animals, and a further series of plain glass for the most part employed as lamps. The art of these beautiful objects is not properly speaking Byzantine, even if at one time the Byzantines were led to imitate their forms. These lamps and vases may have been used at Byzantium, and some of them may even have been manufactured in the Byzantine period after models dating from Late Antiquity. On occasion they were radically "Byzantinized" by adding to the glass vase a silver-gilt fitting with cabochons. Several examples of such work are preserved in the Treasure; details of form and fitting make it clear that these vases were used as lamps suspended on small chains.

One such vase in glass paste of a dark red verging on black calls for special mention. The outer surfaces are covered with gilt ornaments and small polychrome paintings on classical subjects, framed by rosettes; running over the inside of the neck and on the base are imitations of Kufic inscriptions. The paintings are made of enamel colours which, however, were applied in the molten state with a brush and then fixed, as was the gilding on the sides, by a second firing. A silver-gilt mounting, comprising two symmetrical handles, completes the ornamentation of this small vase, a model of sober elegance. At the same time, from the art historical point of view, it is of absorbing interest as reflecting the varied traditions of taste and technique that met and mingled in the industrial arts of Byzantium, for on it we find classical subjects from Greek mythology alongside decorative inscriptions taken over from the Arabs.

Not so long ago this object was absolutely unique of its kind, and even today there is no other to compare with it in respect of its complete and perfect state of preservation. In the course of recent excavations, however, various fragments of Byzantine vases in the same style and technique have come to light in Cyprus, at Corinth, in Transcaucasia and in Russia. This fine glassware must have been manufactured in about the tenth or eleventh century in Constantinople itself, perhaps also at Corinth, and from there exported in all directions.

We may take it for granted that rock crystal, transparent and brilliant as glass but much rarer and costlier, was carved in the Middle Ages at Byzantium, as it had been in Roman times, and also in the workshops, first Persian-Sassanian, then Moslem, of Egypt. Plain, undecorated vessels in rock crystal are very difficult to attribute to any particular country or period. The best characterized of these precious objects preserved in the Treasure of St Mark's are tenth-century works from Fatimid Egypt. Finest of them all, and an unqualified masterpiece, is the ewer with confronted panthers, dated by a Kufic inscription.

Among other rarities in the Treasure are two tall slender vases of veined polychrome marble, whose sole ornament is an animal-shaped handle. These pieces, obviously made in imitation of ancient Oriental vases, can safely be attributed to Byzantium. This attribution is borne out by a similar large vase in serpentine, with two handles in the form of animals' bodies, which is unquestionably a Byzantine work of the tenth century, as is proved by its shape, which is that of vases in the classical tradition

EWER WITH CONFRONTED PANTHERS. ROCK CRYSTAL FROM FATIMID EGYPT. TENTH CENTURY. TREASURE OF ST MARK'S.

(spherical base and four-lobed orifice), and above all by the reliefs on it representing Christ, the Virgin and saints. An inscription engraved on the edge shows that this vase served as a liturgical chalice.

Objects of this kind go to show the skill and taste with which the art of carving hard, ornamental stone was practised at Byzantium in the course of the Middle Ages. Further examples, of equally fine workmanship, are provided by a series of chalices —objects particularly important in Venice. In the case of some, both cup and stem are carved in the same stone (onyx, agate, malachite or serpentine); others, though all of a piece, are given a form requiring no stem; still others consist of two parts made of different materials, the cup of hard stone, the stem of gilt silver. The variety of hard stone used in these last, and the resulting variety of colouring, is remarkable. Nearly always the cup is set in a silver-gilt mounting, consisting of a rim running round the lip and connected to the stem by vertical bands, together with one or two handles. These metal strips are everywhere studded with cabochons or rows of pearls, or lettered with enamelled or nielloed inscriptions; or else, in the most highly decorated examples, overlaid with small enamelled plaques. On some, among them the two large chalices offered by a Byzantine emperor named Romanus, probably Romanus II (959-963), an initial ring of these exquisite enamels runs round the upper edge of the cup, while others adorn the base and still others enhance the vertical designs on the side of the cup. The foundation plaque of the enamels is made of gold, as are the minute partitions separating the colours. Each enamel was made separately and afterwards fastened to the chalice. One or two half-length figures are represented on each enamel. Christ and the Apostles with an Orant Virgin occur several times on a chalice, obviously for liturgical reasons. Since each communion was a renewal of the Lord's Supper, the figures on the chalice served as a reminder of the original participants, while the Orant Virgin symbolized the prayers of intercession addressed to God at each Mass, before communion. But other holy personages also appear on other chalices from Constantinople, notably the canonized bishops. Here again the iconography can be accounted for by the liturgical usage of Byzantium, where the bishop of the diocese was commemorated in the procession known as the Great Entrance which precedes the consecration of the species.

Aesthetically speaking, all these chalices are works of the highest refinement. They owe their effect to the skilled combination of rare and costly materials, the emphasis being laid both on the juxtaposition of variously coloured elements and on the regular alternation of motifs. Considered from this angle, each chalice is unique, no other being quite like it in the colouring of the stone and the arrangement of cabochons, pearls and enamels. But as we compare them we come to discern more or less set patterns of decoration continually resorted to, and even a certain industrialization in the ornaments applied, anyhow in works of the eleventh century, those of the tenth being in every case more distinctive and original. As regards the enamels, the most remarkable are those on the two large chalices offered to St Mark's by the Emperor Romanus. The small enamelled images on them are in every way comparable to paintings, and the point deserves to be emphasized, for it was not until the first Byzantine figural enamels appeared towards the end of the ninth century that artists in Western Europe contrived to produce enamels successfully imitating paintings. Nothing of the kind made in the West before that time rises above the level of ornamental plaques, not even the Anglo-Saxon and Carolingian enamels of the early Middle Ages, in which attempts were made to represent the heads of figures. Byzantium alone, it seems, had by the end of the ninth century sufficiently perfected the technique of enamelling to produce successful figural images. To do so required the utmost skill and precision in manipulating the minute, all-important partitions; in mixing and bringing out the different colours, particularly the flesh tints, most difficult of all; and in firing the enamels at just the right temperature and right length of time to obtain the desired shade of each colour.

The figures on the two chalices presented by Romanus, and on a third adorned with full-length portraits of bishops, are superlative examples of the artistry of the master enamellists of Constantinople round about 950. These works, moreover, display the originality of the Byzantine aesthetic as revealed in this new art form unknown in classical antiquity: bright colours so boldly juxtaposed as to seem almost gaudy, an effect peculiar to enamels; a total absence of the third dimension, the exclusion of "space" resulting naturally from the cloisonné technique of enamelling; bearded faces of a type quite foreign to the tradition of classical art, the enamel technique leading inevitably to the accentuation of each feature of face, beard and hair, and thus giving rise to a certain Oriental cast of face. So successful were these enamels that their bright colours, and some of their other characteristics as well, were taken over and incorporated in the Byzantine mosaics and paintings of the Middle Ages.

The Treasure of St Mark's, though exceptionally rich in fine Byzantine chalices, contains only a few patens (that is, the shallow dish on which the Host is laid at the celebration of the Eucharist). This is something of an anomaly, for each chalice should as a matter of course have its corresponding paten. Whatever the explanation, the few remaining Byzantine patens in the Treasure are, as we might expect, designed and executed very much as the chalices are, except that they are seldom embellished with enamels (and when they are, only with a single enamelled medallion in the centre). The small dish of the paten is carved in hard stone, and its mounting consists of a base and a rim of silver gilt, inset with cabochons.

One of the most unusual and intriguing objects preserved in the Treasure is that known in Venice as the "Grotta della Madonna." A composite creation, somewhat puzzling at first sight, it is a work unique of its kind, consisting of a votive crown, a vase carved in rock crystal (forming the "Grotto"), and a gilt bronze statuette of the

BYZANTINE PATEN. ALABASTER WITH ENAMEL MEDALLION REPRESENTING CHRIST BLESSING.
GILT SILVER RIM INSET WITH PEARLS AND PRECIOUS STONES. TENTH OR ELEVENTH CENTURY. TREASURE OF ST MARK'S.

BYZANTINE CHALICE OFFERED BY THE EMPEROR ROMANUS (II ?). CUP OF AGATE, STEM AND MOUNTING OF GILT SILVER, WITH ENAMELS REPRESENTING CHRIST AND THE APOSTLES. TENTH CENTURY. TREASURE OF ST MARK'S.

Virgin. The three component parts were no doubt put together in Venice itself in the thirteenth century. The votive crown, referred to above in connection with a portrait of the Byzantine Emperor Leo VI (cf. page 53), is a Byzantine work datable to about the year 900; it hung originally over an altar, perhaps in the church of San Zaccaria in Venice, which was built by Leo VI. The crown consists of a plain metal ring inset with pearls. Some of the enamels that originally adorned it have been lost. The remaining enamels, however, portray Leo VI (the portrait just referred to) and several Apostles, including St Andrew shown with a long cross in accordance with the peculiar iconography of Constantinople, where he was venerated as a patron saint. All these enamelled portraits stand out against an almost translucid emerald-green background, a distinctive feature of the oldest figural enamels, to be found again on several other very fine examples in the Marcian Library.

Originally this crown hung alone, but it now serves as the base, or stand, of the curious "Grotto" carved in rock crystal before which the Virgin is praying. The latter is a thirteenth-century Venetian imitation of a small Byzantine sculpture, and it was no doubt in order to present it more effectively that it was fastened to the crown of Leo VI and surrounded by the rock crystal "Grotto." The origin of the latter is uncertain, but it might well be Byzantine and date to the early period of Byzantium (fifth or sixth century). It is actually a vase placed upside down and deliberately broken in part so as to show the small figure of the Virgin to better advantage. The crystal sides of the vase are decorated with columns with Ionic capitals; between the columns are shields and trophies. Whatever we may think of the heterogeneous combination of objects forming the "Grotto of the Virgin," it is worth pointing out that two of them, the crown and the rock crystal vase, are unique pieces, the only extant specimens of two types of precious objects which, long ago, enjoyed their hour of success.

Beside the "Grotto of the Virgin" stands another work unique of its kind, appreciably larger, made of silver gilt and looking like the scale model of a building. For a long time it contained a relic of the Blood of Christ, and though heavy and unwieldy it was borne in processions by the patriarch of Venice himself. This reliquary, however, whose upper part has many holes and openings, was no doubt originally designed as an incense-burner for liturgical ceremonies.

The elaborate lanterns and incense-burners wrought by the Byzantine goldsmiths of the Middle Ages, whether for secular or ecclesiastical use, were often given the form of a building. But as time passed their original purpose was sometimes forgotten—and not in Venice alone. An object of the same type is preserved at Aachen; it, too, is shaped like a toy edifice and, on the strength of inscriptions engraved on its silver walls, can be dated to the tenth century and attributed to a workshop in Antioch. These inscriptions explain, furthermore, that in giving a liturgical object the form of a domed edifice in miniature the intention was to allude to Zion (i.e., the House of God) or to

"THE GROTTO OF THE VIRGIN." ROCK CRYSTAL VASE AND GILT BRONZE STATUETTE MOUNTED ON THE CROWN OF THE BYZANTINE EMPEROR
LEO VI (886-912), REPRESENTED IN THE SECOND MEDALLION FROM THE LEFT. TREASURE OF ST MARK'S.

GILT SILVER RELIQUARY IN THE FORM OF A DOMED EDIFICE, WITH TWO FIGURES IN RELIEF PERSONIFYING COURAGE AND INTELLIGENCE. TWELFTH CENTURY. TREASURE OF ST MARK'S.

the Temple of Jerusalem. The same symbolism might be supposed to apply to the miniature edifice in the Treasure of St Mark's. But here, we feel, it was intended rather to imitate the pavilion or kiosk of a palace, for the building is plainly a secular one. The crosses on the four corner towers of the pavilion were added subsequently (and so thoughtlessly that no trouble was taken to add one to the dome in the centre), while the two figures in relief on the small doors are personifications of the worldly virtues of Courage and Intelligence. No less worldly are the small reliefs on the lower walls of the edifice, representing a pair of lovers and a chubby *putto* with his head in a basket (this is a reminiscence of a Bacchic scene). But what must be particularly noted in this connection is the type of architecture imitated by the goldsmiths: a cube-shaped pavilion with four projecting apses, one on each side, roofed with five domes and four pyramidal towers. The shape of the domes and their intricate open-work patterning, together with the pyramidal towers, are inspired by Moslem models, while certain details, such as the battlemented walls running round the entire edifice, bring to mind the Norman architecture of Sicily. This curious object was apparently produced in some workshop—perhaps in Sicily itself—where Byzantine, Islamic and Romanesque currents of influence converged.

The Treasure of St Mark's preserves two works, equally remarkable, which are sometimes assumed to be the covers of Gospel Books. But the image of the archangel Michael, which figures prominently on both, never occurs on the binding of Gospel Books (whose standard forms of decoration we shall have occasion to examine presently when we come to deal with the Byzantine bindings in the Marcian Library). These two pieces of goldsmiths' work adorned with the figure of the archangel Michael may more plausibly be regarded as icons. True, they are not paintings on wood, as is generally the case, but the icon as such is not necessarily bound up with any particular technique. There are icons in mosaic, there are icons carved in stone or raised in repoussé work in gold and silver; still others are enamels on a metal foundation. The two images of the archangel Michael have the form usually given to icons and, like them again, are enclosed in a frame. But, unlike most icons, they combine an unusual variety of techniques: repoussé reliefs in pure gold, some exceptionally fine gold filigree work (the filigreed background of the half-length archangel is probably the most delicate specimen known of such work), cabochons and inlays of coloured stones, and enamels applied to both plane and curving surfaces. These last are rare; indeed, to apply, unerringly, an even coat of enamel colours to a curved or irregular surface (as here, on the face of the standing archangel and the sphere he is holding, and also on the half-length archangel) is the last refinement of the enamellist's art. Again, to spread the enamels over surfaces as extensive as these is a highly delicate operation. These two icons, furthermore, number among the most remarkable pieces of small-scale Byzantine sculpture. The head of the half-length archangel, seen in front view, with its sensitive modelling and the classic purity of the features, or the standing figure accoutred as a warrior, stiff but firm and well shaped—relief work of this order vouches for a long-standing tradition and experience of plastic art. These icons cannot be dated with any degree of certainty, but an attentive study of their various elements inclines us to assign them both to about the year 1000, or to the early eleventh century. And if this is really the case, the quality of the two reliefs becomes particularly noteworthy, for they would have to be regarded as ranking among the finest products of the "renaissance" of the arts that took place at Byzantium in the time of the Macedonian dynasty (867-1056). A breath of inspiration from reliefs of a much earlier age quickens their forms. But the insertion of these enamelled reliefs in a setting combining all the techniques of the sumptuary arts reflects the luxurious taste of the Byzantine "renaissance."

The full-length figure of the archangel Michael as a warrior is enclosed in a contemporary frame decorated with small enamels representing Byzantine warrior saints. These figures (like the archangel himself in fact) are the patron saints of the Byzantine armies. The icon and the frame form one, both as regards the iconographic theme and their religious function. The original frame of the second icon having been lost, it was replaced by a Venetian one to which a series of earlier Byzantine enamels were added. The back of this frame is overlaid with a silver plaque adorned with ornaments and saints' portraits in repoussé which, though Byzantine work, are later (dating to the eleventh or twelfth century) than the icon of the archangel Michael in half-length on the other side.

Opposite the Ducal Palace, on the west side of the Piazzetta, the beautiful sixteenth-century Libreria Vecchia built by Sansovino (and described by John Addington Symonds as "the crowning triumph of Venetian art") houses the Marcian Library. It contains a priceless collection of Gospel Books in Byzantine bindings and Greek illuminated manuscripts. The Venetian library has the choicest collection now existing of Byzantine bindings in wrought gold studded with precious stones. There are five of these, ranging from the late ninth to the fifteenth century. All are remarkable and well preserved; each reveals a different aspect of the art of decorating the front and back covers of the sumptuous binding of a Gospel Book. It would probably be going too far to say that these five bindings taken together illustrate so many stages in the evolution of the covers designed for Byzantine liturgical works; but at least none repeats the patterns to be seen on the others and each interprets in its own way the elements handed down by tradition.

It must be admitted at the outset that we possess today but a very imperfect knowledge of the history of Byzantine binding. Pictures representing a Gospel Book generally show only very simple types of binding, which must of course have been by far the most common; the small size of such pictures in any case made it difficult to represent bindings with figural decorations. But since a few such book covers in ivory have come down to us, we know that bindings with figural decorations did indeed

BYZANTINE ICON WITH THE ARCHANGEL MICHAEL, FULL-LENGTH. REPOUSSÉ RELIEF IN GOLD, WITH ENAMELS. IN THE BORDER, ENAMELS REPRESENTING WARRIOR SAINTS (SIDES) AND CHRIST BETWEEN TWO SAINTS (TOP). TENTH OR ELEVENTH CENTURY. TREASURE OF ST MARK'S.

exist, anyhow in the fifth and sixth centuries, when they were adorned with small reliefs on Christian themes. The Cross and the Lamb, Christ and the Virgin enthroned, in the middle, are surrounded by small Gospel scenes. The Evangelists' symbols and their portraits figure beside some of these scenes, thus helping to link up the decoration of the bindings with the texts which they enclose.

None of the bindings in the Marcian Library corresponds to this type of decoration, which must have been abandoned after the sixth century. But the general design was retained: a central field occupied to begin with by the Christ on one cover and the Virgin on the other, later by the Crucifixion and the Resurrection; and a wide frame enclosing it, occupied either by half-length portraits of Evangelists and Apostles, and other saints, or by small scenes representing the principal events in the Gospel stories.

With two exceptions (the two latest in date), all these bindings include enamels and are usually inset with precious stones and rows of small pearls. The two latest examples, those whose ornamentation is patterned round the Crucifixion and the Harrowing of Hell, consist of repoussé reliefs. In almost every case the front and back covers of the bindings are made of gilt silver-foil laid over a wooden frame. Exceptionally, the back cover of one binding is decorated with small silver plaques patterned with a few geometric designs in niello work or champlevé enamels.

The oldest of the bindings (page 76) has an archaic charm that holds the eye. On each cover is a wide frame of glass paste inlaid in a network of irregular partitions, enhanced by a row of large pearls. The blue-green of the frame sets off the emerald green of the enamelled Cross in the centre of the binding and the enamelled medallions around it. These enamels are of the oldest type (cf. page 58), the type which we noted above on the crown of the Emperor Leo VI, and which goes back to the late ninth or early tenth century. The arms of the Cross are short and broad, growing broader at each extremity. On the front cover is the figure of Christ crucified, on the back cover that of the Orant Virgin. Christ's head has an unforgettable expression of poignant grief; the tunic he is wearing has its origins in the earliest iconography of Palestine. The monograms round the figure of the Virgin evoke the name of the donatrix.

The next in date (page 77) is a masterpiece of the binder's art as practised with impeccable taste in early medieval Byzantium. The enamelled figures stand out on a gold ground inset with a few fine cabochons. The central field, forming an elongated rectangle, is occupied by the figure of Christ, on the front cover, and that of the Virgin on the back cover—long narrow figures of taut design, with noble faces and measured movements, with pink, semi-transparent flesh tints and garments in several beautiful shades of blue spotted with white. Each is framed by medallions containing half-length portraits of saints, in the same technique. This magnificent work can be attributed to the middle of the tenth century.

The decorative design of the two covers of a third binding brings to mind the sixth-century ivories mentioned above. The elements of the decoration (enamels and cabochons), and the figures they enhance, are the same as those on the previous binding. The workmanship, however, is altogether inferior. Though the enamels show an agreeable range of warm colour tints, the design of figures and draperies remains rudimentary; as for the cabochons, one cannot help being surprised at their careless insertion in holes roughly cut in the metal bands. This is jobber's work, but it is probably not much later in date than the previous binding; it may plausibly be assigned to the early eleventh century.

The decorative effect of the two other bindings, the latest in date, is considerably modified by the use of relief work in repoussé, which is the predominant element on the covers of one and the only element of the decoration on the other. The covers of the first binding are still surrounded with enamel medallions, but they now alternate with small scenes in relief. These enamels, however, are technically inferior to the earlier ones; no semi-transparent pastes are employed. Yet some of the vivid brick-reds and also a light blue that appear here for the first time produce a fine effect, particularly fine when the enamels containing them are set off by the metal reliefs beside them. As for the reliefs in repoussé, we have already noted in connection with the two icons of the archangel Michael that these works are not without a certain importance in the history of Byzantine sculpture. But while the two icons of the tenth (or perhaps of the eleventh) century are works of almost monumental sculpture, the scenes in repoussé on the two reliefs of the fourteenth and fifteenth centuries have both the qualities and the shortcomings of sculpture on a very small scale so common in goldsmiths' work. To say this is not to belittle the very real excellence of their workmanship, which in the modelling of heads and draperies shows a renewed interest in antique sculpture and at the same time the unmistakable influence of painting, or more exactly of miniature painting which had transmitted from generation to generation the conventional schemes of the Gospel scenes. These are treated in the same way in manuscript illuminations, on icons, and in goldsmiths' work. There is moreover an obvious similarity between the design of a Byzantine binding of the fourteenth century, like those in the Marcian Library, and the design of an icon of the same period when placed within a figural setting. For these settings consist of a ground of gilt silver-foil against which are represented, in repoussé relief, small portraits of saints or Gospel scenes, their sequence roughly corresponding to the sequence of the great Feasts of the Church.

By the end of the Byzantine period the old diversity of usages and traditions, the old variety of types and forms, and even of techniques, was largely a thing of the past. The field of artistic expression had been steadily narrowed down, and artists seldom ventured to depart from their small stock of set formulas and familiar motifs, adapting them to all occasions. This art was narrower and more monotonous than that of earlier ages, but it gained in cohesion what it lost in the way of freshness and freedom.

COVER OF A BYZANTINE GOSPEL BOOK. CRUCIFIXION, IN ENAMELS, SURROUNDED BY ENAMEL MEDALLIONS OF SAINTS AND ANGELS RINGED WITH
PEARLS, WITHIN A WIDE BORDER OF GLASS PASTE. NINTH OR TENTH CENTURY. COD. LAT. I, 101, MARCIAN LIBRARY.

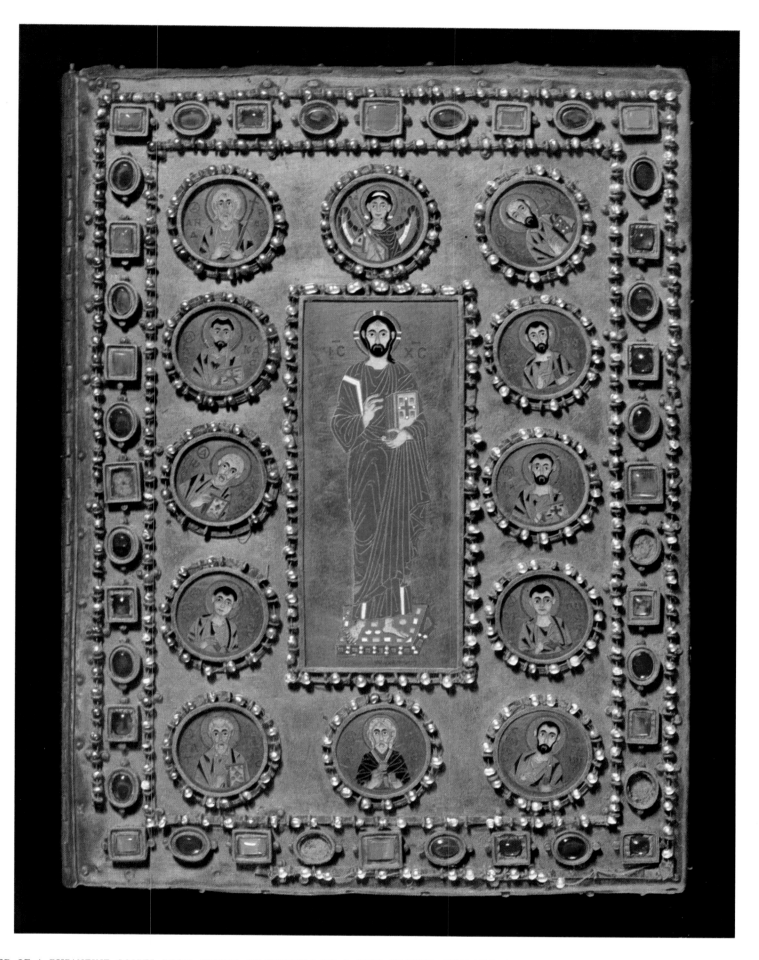

COVER OF A BYZANTINE GOSPEL BOOK. CHRIST, IN ENAMELS ON A GOLD GROUND, SURROUNDED BY ENAMEL MEDALLIONS OF SAINTS RINGED WITH PEARLS, WITHIN A BORDER OF PRECIOUS STONES. MID-TENTH CENTURY. COD. LAT. I, 100, MARCIAN LIBRARY.

A brief survey cannot do justice to the rich collection of illuminated Byzantine manuscripts in the Marcian Library, but it has the advantage of concentrating our attention on the finest volumes and on a few illuminated pages of outstanding quality. One such volume is a Psalter, or Book of Psalms, which belonged to or was ordered by the Byzantine Emperor Basil II, conqueror of the Bulgarians (in 1017). The Emperor is represented on the frontispiece in the uniform of a Byzantine general, surrounded by the warrior saints whose favour enabled him to triumph over his enemies. He is shown being crowned by God, while an angel hands him his spear; grovelling at his feet, in abject obeisance, are a group of Bulgarian nobles. The Emperor's portrait, with the strong rhythm of the movements and the ringing harmony of the colours, is by no means lacking in purely aesthetic qualities. It offers an example, furthermore, of the way in which the great events of contemporary Byzantine history were, characteristically, transposed into pictorial formulas in the classical tradition. This stern, awe-inspiring image—no doubt reflecting an age of equally fierce realities—strikes a contrast with the suave style of the paintings which, on the following pages of the manuscript, tell the story of King David, who wrote the Psalms. Such a contrast is by no means unusual in Byzantine art.

Profane and secular figures—acrobats, dancing girls, personifications of the Months and Virtues—have found their way into the pages of a Gospel Book, where they serve to decorate and enliven the Canon Tables. It was from the art of Late Antiquity that the Byzantine masters took over this practice of introducing a certain number of secular subjects into an otherwise purely religious work. Architectural designs were generally used to frame the Canon Tables (i.e., the tables referring to passages in the different Gospels which deal with the same subject or episode), and it was here that secular themes were felt to be a not inappropriate adornment. The architectural elements themselves imitate the light open pavilions and summer houses of gardens; the fountains and trees beside them, and the birds and animals playing among them, evoke parks and pleasure gardens, and in this half-real, half-imaginary setting various personifications are represented. Paintings of this kind are in much the same vein, and executed with much the same verve, as the mosaics in King Roger's room in the palace at Palermo, with their trees, peacocks, wild animals and hunters. As we see them here, in the opening pages of a Gospel Book, they provide undoubted evidence of the penetration of Court art into the domain of Church art.

A third illuminated manuscript, this time a non-religious work, reveals another, highly interesting aspect of Byzantine secular painting. The illustrations in this manuscript are an interpretation by an eleventh-century Byzantine artist of an illuminated treatise on hunting and fishing, by Pseudo-Oppian, originally illustrated about the third or fourth century A.D. The text is closely followed by the pictures, very small ones but very numerous, showing animals, hunting scenes, the trapping and capture of different birds and quadrupeds, and also illustrating the methods of fishing described

PSALTER OF THE BYZANTINE EMPEROR BASIL II, FRONTISPIECE: PORTRAIT OF BASIL II (976-1025).
EARLY ELEVENTH CENTURY. COD. GR. Z. 17, FOLIO 3 RECTO, MARCIAN LIBRARY.

in the treatise. Most of the paintings in the Venice manuscript are faithful copies of the prototypes, in the classical style, in the earlier manuscript. Some of them, however, seem to have been recast or reinterpreted by the medieval painter, who either misunderstood his model or deliberately transformed it, even to the extent of entirely replacing it by something else of his own devising. But on the whole this branch of Byzantine secular art—the illustration of "scientific" books—keeps closely to classical models and has little if anything original to show.

Byzantine religious painting in the Middle Ages, in the domain of book illumination, was of course also based on models created in the first centuries after the Peace of the Church. But those models were not followed so systematically here as they were in secular or scientific paintings, for while scientific studies made little or no progress in the Byzantine period, the dogmas and iconography of the Christian religion were the central preoccupation of those whose task it was to supervise the activities of painters and artists. Theologians, liturgists, preachers and even laymen were constantly busy writing commentaries on the Holy Scriptures, and these could not be ignored by religious painters. The bulk and scope of this work of exegesis naturally varied from one book of the Bible to another. Most commentators applied themselves to expounding the four Gospels; it was these, too, that were most often interpreted in pictures. As for the Old Testament, it was only partially illustrated, different books often being interpreted in an entirely different spirit. Thus the Book of Job, of which the Marcian Library possesses a remarkable illuminated manuscript of the tenth century, is peculiar in that it remained outside the main stream of Christian iconography. Each illuminator, moreover, tempered his work with elements drawn from his own surroundings, or from the arts with which he was familiar, and so gave it an accent of his own. We find, for example, illuminated copies of the Book of Job in Greek which are wholly classical in inspiration (such manuscripts reflect the oldest versions of these text illustrations), while others are interpreted in an outright Gothic style. The Job manuscript in the Marcian Library, being one of the oldest, is therefore more purely classical than most of the others. The beautiful figures of Job's friends, standing beside him and pursuing their interminable discussions, bear the imprint of antique paintings. To see how true this is, it is enough to note the drapery folds and the rhythmic movements of the figures. To this, the Byzantine illuminator of the Middle Ages could generally add little more than a certain linear schematism and the expressive outline, of which he was so fond, which isolates each human figure against the unrelieved emptiness of the monochrome backgrounds.

The illuminated Byzantine manuscripts commented on above represent but a small, considered selection among the finest of those preserved in the Marcian Library. There are others, notably among the Gospel Books illustrated with Evangelist portraits and vignettes, which give us a good idea of the usual type of fine book produced at Byzantium in the eleventh and twelfth centuries. The founder of a church, for example, or the benefactor of a monastery, would present to the sanctuary he had endowed a Gospel Book illustrated in this manner, and it was likely to be used by the officiating clergy day in, day out, for many generations. At Byzantium, in the Middle Ages, new churches were frequently being founded, generally quite small ones, which did not have sufficient means to keep a stock of liturgical books on hand, much less a fine library of them, as was the case in the great churches of the Latin West. Indeed, the freshness, the unblemished perfection with which some of the best Carolingian manuscripts are still preserved today is astonishing—the reason being of course that they were seldom opened, and never in daily use as were Byzantine Gospel Books, even the finest of them.

Several illuminated Byzantine manuscripts of note are preserved in the Treasure of the Greek church of San Giorgio dei Greci, just off the Riva degli Schiavoni. Kept in the small museum beside the church, these manuscripts can now be consulted there. One of them is a sumptuous Gospel Book, but of a particular type, with tiny margin illustrations. Here again, as in so much goldsmiths' work, the desired effect depends

TREATISE ON HUNTING AND FISHING BY PSEUDO-OPPIAN.
PAGE ILLUSTRATING METHODS OF FISHING. ELEVENTH CENTURY.
COD. GR. Z. 479, FOLIO 59 RECTO, MARCIAN LIBRARY.

on the finesse and delicacy of the execution, in other words on consummate crafts-manship. Another illuminated manuscript at San Giorgio, dating to the very end of the Byzantine period, is a non-religious work, the *Story of Alexander the Macedonian* by Pseudo-Callisthenes. These book paintings, of a kind extremely rare, are of the highest interest as showing us what the Byzantine illustrators of the late Middles Ages were capable of making of antique models of secular painting on a literary theme.

In the small museum of the church of San Giorgio dei Greci—and also in the picture gallery of the Academy—we find examples of the last category of Byzantine works of art that will be dealt with here: wooden icons. The oldest of these paintings go back to the last two centuries of the Byzantine Empire (that is, the thirteenth and fourteenth), but most of them date to the fifteenth, sixteenth and seventeenth centu-ries. Some were brought from continental Greece and the Aegean islands; others were made in Venice itself, at Padua, and elsewhere in Italy, either by Greek painters or by their Italian disciples. Certain of these icons, including some very large ones, formed part of an iconostasis; others hung on the walls of private houses. The most famous example of these paintings is in the Academy. It consists of a whole ensemble of very delicate images covering both sides of a large wooden cross of the fifteenth century. This cross belonged to Cardinal Bessarion (1403-1472), the famous Greek churchman who settled in Italy and at his death bequeathed his great library to Venice, where it now forms part of the Marciana. In Venice, throughout the Middle Ages and long after, Greek icons were commonly employed as devotional images, as distinct from paintings on religious themes. It is said that Titian had one in his private apartments.

It was to this semi-Oriental custom, and to the private piety that ensured its conti-nuance, that the art of the icon, in the strict Byzantine tradition, owed its long survival in Venice and the Adriatic region of Italy. To be sure, it was overshadowed by the extraordinary rise of Italian painting in the Renaissance, but it did not die out. The art of the icon, as we see it in these Venetian works, may lack spontaneity, but it casts the mind back in time to the age when it flourished in the Byzantine East, from whence it was brought to Venice and there preferred to any other iconographic expres-sion of the Christian verities. Many minor painters of the late Middle Ages, and even some of the Quattrocento, whether intentionally or not, made borrowings from Byzantine icons and mosaics, and this art was one at least of the influences that went to determine that specific colouring which we associate with the great Venetian paintings of the Cinquecento.

THE DUCAL PALACE

3

ART AS AN INSTRUMENT OF POWER: THE DUCAL PALACE

The earliest extant records describe the Doges' Palace, or Ducal Palace, as a towered castle with high walls, defended on all sides by a deep moat. Here the military commander, the Doge of Venice (from the Latin *dux*, meaning leader), entrenched himself with his men to defend the city against enemy attack. "No enemy force ever made bold to scale those walls which they knew to be manned by soldiers who, though few, were resolute and warlike." Such is the entry we read in the chronicle of John the Deacon for the year 977.

The early settlers, driven from the mainland by the barbarian invasions, brought with them to the lagoons the mainland practice of building towers and castles to protect the community from attack. The very name of Torcello (Torricellum) and that of one of the six wards of Venice itself (Castello) bear witness to the survival of this practice in the islands. To prevent enemy ships from forcing their way into the city, the Venetians stretched iron chains by night across the water between two towers on opposite banks of the Grand Canal, at the point where it is joined by the Rio delle Torricelle, a small canal which takes its name from the two towers.

In those days the Ducal Palace was no different from any other fortified castle of the Middle Ages, with its plain, undecorated façade and windowless walls; a single gate, protected by a drawbridge, gave access to the palace. The contrast with the palace we see today could not be more complete: everywhere graceful arcades and loggias; no break of continuity between the squares outside and the spacious interior; everywhere decorations and a wealth of colour; the delicate crenellation at the top of the façade, never meant for defence, brings to mind a classical frieze or the ornamental patterning of Arab edifices. All the features of this architecture—indeed, of this new style, bound up with a new and unforeseen *idea* of Venice—are the outcome and reflection of a political and spiritual situation very different from that in which Venice found herself in early times.

As we look back over the course of Venetian history and try to single out the time when so momentous a change occurred, when Venice, instead of a grim fortress closed in upon herself, became the open city we know today—as we thus turn the pages of Venetian history we may be led to pause over the name of one of her greatest Doges: Sebastiano Ziani. He was the head of the government from September 29, 1172, to April 13, 1178, when, as an old man, he abdicated and withdrew to the monastery of San Giorgio Maggiore. From there he could see, outspread before his eyes, the city to which he had given a new lease of life. Sebastiano Ziani was the thirty-ninth Doge of Venice; several centuries, then, had had to elapse before the city, its early hardships surmounted, became conscious of itself as a sea power and came to assume a distinctive form of its own, both in its outward aspect and in its internal structure.

The terrors of the early Middle Ages had gradually come to an end, and with them the fear of attack and invasion. The chains barring the canals were withdrawn, the moats were filled. Venice no longer needed walls, towers and drawbridges to defend herself. Doge Ziani, bold and high-spirited, led his countrymen aboard their light ships into the open sea, far from their homes in the Lagoon, there to waylay the enemy. Under his leadership the Venetian fleet became the bulwark of the city, its front line of defence and security.

"The city walled by the sea, with open gates unafraid," sang the poet Pietro de Natali. For centuries Venice relied on this defensive strategy, nor indeed has any city been so effectively impregnable and enjoyed security so long. Down to the fall of the Republic (on May 12, 1797) she maintained her independence and integrity, unique in the world in never having been invaded, much less occupied, by any of her enemies. So that once having achieved settled government, once having built up her sea power, she pursued a steady course in the guiding light of her own past, modifying her internal structure as little as possible.

The same is true of her architecture which, in point of fact, might well be called after Sebastiano Ziani. For it was under his leadership that it assumed the features which, beneath the variety of ornaments and styles, reappear century after century. Lightly built walls broken by arcades and galleries, richly decorated and richly coloured, became the norm of Venetian architecture, and never failed to stimulate the imagination of Venetian builders; for these qualities answered perfectly to the spirit of the city, extrovert and peace-loving. To Sebastiano Ziani goes the credit not only of rebuilding the Ducal Palace and setting the standards of Venetian architecture, but also of replanning the whole layout of the city and giving it the organic structure which it retains to this day. It was he, too, who had the two columns erected on the Piazzetta, which go to form a gateway to the city, henceforth open to the traffic of the world, and the commencement of a kind of Sacred Way leading from the landing place on the Lagoon to the Ducal Palace and St Mark's.

A special ordinance (also attributed to Ziani) enjoined the masters of Venetian ships to bring with them, on their return voyage, building material, works of art, and stones of every kind. Hence the arrival in Venice of a fragment of a statue representing Alexander, from Greece, and a bronze lion from Persia; in myth-creating Venice these two works, once they were placed on top of the two columns in the Piazzetta, came to represent St Mark and St Theodore, patron saints and religious symbols of the city. Carved in the monolithic blocks supporting the columns are personifications of the Arts and Crafts—an allusion to the patriotic spirit of solidarity and fellowship which reigned among the working people of Venice, who very early were organized in corporations or trade guilds, which maintained the efficiency of the members and the high quality of Venetian manufactures, prevented the divulgence of trade secrets and ensured a just remuneration for all concerned.

To Doge Sebastiano Ziani, as to the founders of all nations, every merit and every achievement was attributed by later ages. Many features of this great historical figure remain indistinct, but the veneration of his countrymen converted his every enterprise and every alleged purpose into glorious deeds. Undoubtedly, however, it was thanks to Ziani that by the eighth decade of the twelfth century Venice was equal to the exacting honour of acting as host to Pope Alexander III and the Emperor Frederick Barbarossa, who were then engaged in their great struggle for the leadership of Europe. After peace had been made between them in neutral Venice, a peace sealed by ceremonies and festivals which remained famous in the annals of the Republic, Doge Ziani and Barbarossa accompanied the Pope on his homeward journey as far as Ancona.

These events are supposed to have taken place in the early days of August, 1177, and to this year date almost all the political legends glorifying Venice: the Battle of Salvore, the Mystical Wedding of Venice with the Sea, etc. One of these legends tells how the Doge of Venice was officially acknowledged as possessing authority equal to that of Pope and Emperor. The people of Ancona—so the legend goes—having prepared for their illustrious guests two symbolic umbrellas, emblematic of royal authority, Pope Alexander commanded them to prepare another for the Doge, because he represented the Republic of Venice, which was then considered the third power in Europe, after the papacy and the empire.

In every ceremony the Doge was accordingly invested with imperial pomp and in no case was it permitted for him to be placed on a footing inferior to that of the princes and potentates received by him in Venice. His titles, flattering to the pride and vanity of every Venetian, were deferentially acknowledged by the greatest monarchs of East and West: Hypatos and Protospatharius; Most Illustrious, Most Excellent, Most Serene Highness; Duke of Venice, Dalmatia and Croatia; and Lord and Master of a quarter and a half-quarter of the Roman Empire. His every gesture and every particular of his dress came to have a precise significance attaching to it. His tunic

VIEW OF THE PIAZZETTA FROM THE LAGOON, WITH THE LIBRERIA VECCHIA (LEFT), ST MARK'S (CENTRE) AND THE DUCAL PALACE (RIGHT). IN THE FOREGROUND, THE COLUMNS OF ST THEODORE AND ST MARK.

trimmed with ermine was the appanage of princes. His red hose and red shoes indicated that he had been knighted by the Byzantine Emperor. His mantle with a train held by two train bearers was similar to those worn by Alexander III and Frederick Barbarossa when they met in Venice in 1177. The familiar horned cap of the Doges—the principal emblem of the ducal office, kept in the Treasure of St Mark's and brought out only on occasions of great ceremony—was richly jewelled with sixty-six pearls, diamonds and emeralds and a single ruby alone worth twenty-five thousand ducats.

When on fixed days the Doge came forth from the palace to take part in some procession or ceremony, he was always accompanied by all the emblems of his office and authority: "a state umbrella was held over him, lighted tapers were borne by his side, trumpets blared and banners waved." The ostentation surrounding him, his sceptre, his stool, his cushion and other regalia, exalted in the person of the Doge the might and grandeur of Venice. At the head of the procession flew eight gold-embroidered banners of silk (those bestowed on Doge Ziani by Alexander III): first came the red banners if the Republic was at war, the white if it was at peace; green ones indicated a truce, blue an alliance.

VIEW OF ST MARK'S SQUARE. FROM LEFT TO RIGHT: THE PROCURATIE NUOVE (1586-1640), THE NAPOLEONIC WING (1810), AND THE PROCURATIE VECCHIE (1500-C. 1532).

It was one of the Doge's principal duties, and one of his highest responsibilities, to act as guardian of the relics of St Mark: *"Solus patronus et verus gubernator ecclesiae Sancti Marci."* This function invested him with particular ecclesiastical powers and in certain circumstances he could pronounce a benediction. This contributed in no small degree to sanctify his person and enhance his prestige.

Some of the more conservative senators at one time proposed to transfer the seat of the Doge—which had always been in the Ducal Palace—to an outlying position beyond the Rio di Palazzo. They were afraid the Doge might be tempted, by his authority and his central position in the city, to make himself absolute master of the State and transform the Republic into a monarchy. But so strict were the organs of control and supervision surrounding the Doge, so clearly defined were his rights and powers, that he was effectively prevented from abusing an authority for which he was held strictly accountable, and not in his lifetime only. At the death of every Doge three magistrates were chosen by the Great Council, called the "Inquisitors upon the Deceased Doge." It was their business to hold an official inquiry into all the dead man's actions and to establish whether or not, in the discharge of his office, he had observed all the obligations contained in the "Ducal Promise" *(Promissione Ducale)*, to which he had sworn on the day of his election. "If the Inquisitors found," writes a Florentine historian, "that the deceased Doge had in any wise done amiss, they were bound to bring accusation against him. And whatsoever fine he thus incurred was imposed on his heirs."

The political wisdom of the Venetians, with its fund of customs and laws, its involved, carefully regulated ceremonials, wove so intricate a system of checks and balances round the Doge as to make him merely the servant and spokesman of the government; he came increasingly to be a kind of figurehead, an embodiment of the idea of the State. The outward show attaching to his office was calculated to contribute to this end; every ceremony was designed to exalt, in the public eye, the triumph of the State in his person. "The Lords of Venice, though they have no authority, have majesty; for while it is well to be without the first, it is unwise to be without the second," wrote Machiavelli. Architectural forms and types of coinage, the hierarchy of the state, the protocol observed in ceremonies, the administration of justice, oratory, poetry and the figurative arts—all tended to enhance the prestige of the Doge, the living symbol of the Republic of St Mark. What ceremonies are to be compared with those that took place in the church, where the Doge was solemnly consecrated and then came forth, as in an ancient Triumph, to be carried round the square amid the acclamations of the people, to whom he threw gold and silver coins by the handful? What prince had a nobler seat than the Doge, as he sat in state between the bronze horses on the open gallery of St Mark's—a sight seen and recorded by Petrarch—and watched the tournaments and pageants in the square below? What throne more regal than the Bucentaur, the gilded barge of State?

VIEW OF THE DUCAL PALACE. THE FAÇADES IN THEIR PRESENT FORM DATE FROM THE LATE FOURTEENTH AND **EARLY FIFTEENTH CENTURY**.
IN THE FOREGROUND, COLUMN IN THE PIAZZETTA WITH THE LION OF ST MARK.

Equally impressive is the Giants' Staircase, in the Ducal Palace, where, at the head of the stairs, thirty-seven Doges were solemnly crowned. It was built for the express purpose of providing a suitable public place for the coronation ceremony, which had hitherto been held in private. The decree, dated November 11, 1485, reads as follows. "Since the principal insignia of our Most Serene Prince is the ducal cap worn on his head, it behoves us to give a fit and proper form to the ceremony during which this insignia is conferred on him. No longer must our Doges be crowned, as hitherto, in secret and by private hands, without decorum and indeed in contempt of the ducal dignity. His coronation must take place publicly and solemnly. We therefore ordain and decree: that the future Doge and all his successors, after being elected and having received the standard of St Mark in the Basilica, and after being borne round the Square, shall return to the Palace and take the oath of office on the staircase. Immediately after the oath has been sworn, the youngest Councillor shall place the sacred veils on the head of his Serene Highness and the senior Councillor shall then invest him with the Ducal Cap, pronouncing these words only: Receive the crown of the Dukedom of Venice."

From the Arco Foscari the statues of Adam and Eve, carved by Antonio Rizzo, look towards the Giants' Staircase from their niches, as if representing mankind at large and in that capacity witnessing the coronation and triumph of each successive Doge. The Staircase rises in the very heart of the "Palatium," deriving from ancient models, which, besides the Doge's apartments, included the court of honour and different arcaded squares, government buildings, commemorative monuments and places set aside for worship The Porta della Carta forms a triumphal arch giving access to the Palace, which was both a Parliament and a royal residence. The Foscari Monument (Arco Foscari) was erected to the Chief of State; at the top are represented the Virtues necessary for good government. In the Ducal Palace, as in the palaces of the Late Roman and Byzantine emperors, are loggias and galleries, an armoury, an arsenal, a museum, private apartments, and archives. Stately stairways lead to the halls where the councils and tribunals met, and give access to the residential area, to the galleries and balconies.

Among the buildings which in course of time sprang up round the Ducal Palace, are the Procuratie, seat of the high government officials known as Procurators; the Granaries, where reserves were stored for the lean years when harvests failed; the Prisons (besides a political prison in the empty space beneath the Giants' Staircase), for the laws were severe and the Venetian government brooked no infraction of its authority.

This corner of the Ducal Palace, facing the Lagoon, suggests the prow of a great ship. The statue above the column represents the Archangel Michael with a drawn sword, the personification of Divine Justice. Beneath it, on the lower arcade (visible in the photograph on page 91), is the sculpture of Adam and Eve representing the Fall of Man. The Palace is built of Istrian limestone and Verona marble, the characteristic materials of all Venetian architecture. The two windows are those of the Hall of the Great Council.

SOUTH-WEST CORNER OF THE DUCAL PALACE, BETWEEN THE PIAZZETTA AND THE LAGOON.

In 1176, under Doge Sebastiano Ziani, St Mark's Square was sufficiently enlarged, by filling in the Rio Batario canal, to enable the entire population to take part in the public ceremonies held there. It was in the time of Doge Ziani, too, that the square was first surrounded by porticoes and loggias, perhaps in imitation of the great Roman theatres in Verona, Pola and other ancient towns in the vicinity of Venice. The square was adorned on all sides with the trophies of Venetian victories.

As always in Venice, each element of the new constructions was rich in connotations and allusions—religious and moral, historical and political, literary, aesthetic and environmental. But each of them had to answer first of all to the requirements of public utility. The Venetians expected that the purpose of a given edifice and the function of its forms should stand clearly revealed at a glance. It was left to the genius of the architect to find the solutions best adapted to the necessities of the moment —at one time, for example, the policy of peaceful expansion laid down by Ziani, at another the need to enlarge the seat of government.

The members of the supreme assembly of the State, numbering three hundred and seventeen in 1264, increased in less than forty years to over a thousand. A decree of July 14, 1301, reads: "As the Hall of the Great Council is no longer adequate to house the members of the Council, it is hereby decreed that the said Hall shall be enlarged." For this it was necessary to rebuild the Ducal Palace. Over the arcades and loggias of Ziani's Palace, the genius of an unknown architect translated this bald decree into gracefully soaring forms and raised the light yet grandiose walls of the Great Council Hall. As seen from outside, those walls are broken and modulated by inlays of coloured marble and the contrasting play of light and shadow set up by the broad windows. For this is an architecture in which pictorial values are fully brought out. Most remarkable of all, and a tribute to the imaginative power of the architect, is the fact that the great cube formed by the added storey, with the smooth mass of its walls, in no way overburdens the two lower storeys with their open arcades and light supporting columns. This arrangement—the lighter storeys below, the heavier above—is not so paradoxical as it seems when we realize that, colouristically, the double row of arcades with their deep pools of shadow convey a greater density and weight than the vast wall surfaces above, radiant with light.

The balconied window on the façade facing the Lagoon (the Sea Façade, as Ruskin called it) was the prototype of a thousand balconies in the city, serving as a model for sculptors and artists such as Jacopo Bellini. It was designed by Pier Paolo and Jacobello Dalle Masegne, following the decree issued by the Senate on July 22, 1400, to the effect that, "for the honour of the Dominion and the City," the Ducal Palace too should be provided with a balcony, such a one as might fulfil the same political function as the balconies of Roman and Byzantine palaces, where the ruler appeared before the people as the exalted personification of the power of the State. The balconied windows

VENETIAN GOTHIC ART OF THE FIRST HALF OF THE FIFTEENTH CENTURY: THE DRUNKENNESS OF NOAH. HIGH RELIEF IN ISTRIAN LIMESTONE.
SOUTH-EAST CORNER OF THE DUCAL PALACE, BESIDE THE PONTE DELLA PAGLIA.

FLORENTINE ART OF THE FIFTEENTH CENTURY: THE JUDGMENT OF SOLOMON. HIGH RELIEF IN ISTRIAN LIMESTONE.
NORTH-WEST CORNER OF THE DUCAL PALACE, NEAR THE PORTA DELLA CARTA.

then, both on the Sea Façade and the Piazzetta Façade, the Giants' Staircase, and indeed the whole Palace, were designed to fulfil certain very definite functions; and their architecture and ornamentation were strictly determined by those functions.

It sometimes happened that a building was put up purely for the sake of political prestige; the Clock Tower, for example, on the north side of St Mark's Square. The funds necessary for its construction were allocated by the government at a time when Venice was at war, "lest it should appear to our enemies that the Republic were drained of its resources." Wealthy citizens at all times contributed greatly to the splendour of Venice by building stately and palatial houses. And this was even truer of the great religious associations and confraternities called Schools *(Scuole)*, which were always ready to spend large sums of money to do honour to their city and state.

No other city or country attached so much importance as Venice did to beautifying the seat of its government. (Think, for example, of the grim civic fortresses of Florence and Siena.) On the Ducal Palace, both inside and out, was lavished a profusion of ornaments and decorations which elsewhere—particularly in France—were usually reserved for the cathedral. The chief aim of all these decorations was that of educating the people to respect the law, of developing their civic pride and preparing them by degrees to assume social responsibilities.

The Ducal Palace, in addition to being the Parliament House and the residence of the Chief of State, was also the seat of the courts of law. Hence its further significance in the eyes of the Venetians as a Temple of Justice. Statues of Justice stand over the two great balconied windows on the Sea and Piazzetta façades, and over the Porta della Carta. On the right of the entrance known as the Porta del Frumento (the main gate of the Palace in the time of Doge Ziani) is represented Solomon (*"Rex sum justicie"*). On the columns at the three corners of the Palace—key points both of its structure and its symbolism—are represented three examples of divine and human justice: the Angel punishing Adam; Noah, a just man and therefore saved from the Flood; and the Judgment of Solomon, which stands above the capital on which the most famous legislators of antiquity are portrayed. A bas-relief on the Piazzetta Façade represents the figure of Justice, with sword and scales, seated on a lion-throne and trampling on the symbols of military insurrection and civil disturbance; inscribed on the background of the relief is the word VENETIA, indicating that justice in that city is synonymous with the very effigy and emblem of Venice herself.

The whole city and its commercial life were based on the principles of justice and fair dealing. On the church of San Giacomo di Rialto, reputedly the oldest religious edifice in Venice, is the following inscription: *Hoc circa templum sit jus mercantibus aequum, pondera nec vergant, nec sit conventio prava* ("Around this temple may the merchants' law be just, weights fair and contracts equitable").

97

GIOVANNI AND BARTOLOMEO BON: THE PORTA DELLA CARTA (1438-1441), MAIN ENTRANCE OF THE DUCAL PALACE.
LEFT, THE PILLARS OF ACRE AND THE FOUR TETRARCHS. RIGHT (ON LOWER ARCADE), THE JUDGMENT OF SOLOMON.

BALCONIED WINDOW ON THE PIAZZETTA FAÇADE OF THE DUCAL PALACE. 1536.

The structure of the Republic was likened by the Florentine Donato Giannotti and other older writers to that of a pyramid. "The foundation and basis on which the whole Republic of Venice stands is the Great Council, on which all other organs depend and which includes all citizens whose age and birthright entitles them to sit on it . . . Then, as the pyramid narrows, comes the Council of the Pregadi, or Senate; this is followed by the Collegio, or Cabinet, where the pyramid narrows still more, for it is this Cabinet that counsels and governs the whole Republic. Finally, at the summit of the pyramid, is the Doge." Another early observer writes admiringly of "this Republic of the Venetians, strongly united in its members, which seems in truth to form a pyramid." In the compact and unified world of that Republic, whose rulers seemed all-knowing in their steady efficiency and far-seeing calculations, long-term policies were pursued with an unswerving tenacity impossible in governments subject to ministerial and dynastic changes. Even religion came to be invested with specific local values which, by the very fact of his being born in Venice, were early impressed on the mind of every citizen.

While in the church of St Mark's (always a living link between Venice and the past) nearly every ornament was imported from some distant land and bore the impress of its original civilization, in the Ducal Palace everything was expressly and specifically made for the Palace and reflects the Venetian genius. Each element here may well strike us as necessary and matchless, for each, over and above its intrinsic beauty, fulfils both a spiritual function and a didactic purpose. Take the sculptured capitals of the lower arcade (those of the gallery above represent saints and symbols of the "heavenly city," in opposition to the "earthly city" below). They represent the arts and crafts, the races and peoples of many lands, birds and animals, figures of ancient sages and emperors, the activities of man and the signs of the Zodiac that govern them, the products of the months and seasons; this, in short, is a *speculum mundi*, representing the vices and virtues and holding up the noble example of famous men.

None of these carvings is particularly Venetian in style or character. Gradually, however, as we enter the Palace by way of the appointed places where the principal ceremonies of State were solemnized (the Porta della Carta, the Giants' Staircase, and the Golden Staircase) and proceed towards the more private and secluded chambers, we meet with themes increasingly pointed and specific in their purport, clearly intended to glorify Venice and educate its citizens. The culmination comes with the representation of *Paradise* in the Hall of the Great Council, an other-worldly vision and apotheosis of the earthly city called by Aretino "almost an image of Paradise."

The difficulties of attaining to the highest offices of state are intimated, at the very entrance to the Palace, by two baskets of fruit carved at the foot of the Giants' Staircase: they contain medlars, thus alluding to a popular Italian proverb to the effect that "time and patience ripen all." As to those to whom it was given to sit in

COURTYARD OF THE DUCAL PALACE. FROM LEFT TO RIGHT: THE CLOCK FAÇADE (1603-1614), THE ARCO FOSCARI (1450-1470),
THE GIANTS' STAIRCASE (1485-1521), AND THE EAST WING OF THE DUCAL PALACE.
UPPER LEFT, DOME OF THE SOUTH TRANSEPT OF ST MARK'S.

the council chambers of the Ducal Palace and guide the destinies of Venice, the moving spirit behind their daily deliberations was well summed up in a phrase uttered by one of them, Marin Sanudo (1466-1535), a member of the Great Council, whose Diary is one of the great source books of Venetian history. "I pray for the grace of God," he wrote, "that my actions in the Senate may be to the benefit of my country."

When Pier Soderini, inspired by the reforming spirit of Savonarola, embarked on an experiment in democracy in Florence, in 1495, and sought to lay the foundations of a republic, he modelled the new government on that of Venice. Even in redecorating the Palazzo Vecchio the Florentines followed the example set by the unified historical vision of the paintings with which the Venetians had decorated their seat of government. Indeed, the Hall of the Great Council was considered the prototype and pattern of political iconography in all the capitals of Baroque Europe. The Venetians owed this admiring homage not only to the longevity and efficiency of their machinery of government, but also to the fact that at each period of their history they had tact and insight enough to decorate their Ducal Palace with works both eminently appropriate and universally appealing. The ingenuous didacticism, the mystical and religious themes current in medieval times, soon gave place to the glorification of signal events or legends in Venetian history, such in particular as bore directly on the political development of the Republic. Later came the classical iconography revived by the Humanists, and more and more painters turned for inspiration to emblems and mythology. But the preference always went to themes connected with the history of Venice, as is shown by the opposition sometimes met with when allegorical fantasies were represented instead of the exploits of national heroes. If a religious element enters into some of these secular and historical scenes, its purpose is to impart an added eloquence to the subject.

The Ducal Palace accordingly presents an inexhaustible accumulation of artistic and political experience recorded in every detail of its architecture and decoration—experience such as can still be appreciated today despite the distance at which we stand from the myths embodied in it. The very stones of this monument, which tell of the heyday of Venice and her imperial state, were once regarded by Venetians with a love and respect that verged on idolatry. One may perhaps smile today at the quaint and earnest pages of Sansovino in which the Senators stand opposed to the renovation of the Ducal Palace after it had been gutted by fire, and insist on having the surviving walls preserved at all costs. "This most noble palace having been founded under the happiest auspices by our fathers and their forebears, the Republic has accordingly from that time forward steadily grown in power and greatness, and has become the foremost in the world..." In the same way, when in 1599 the church of San Giacomo di Rialto stood in need of repairs, it was solemnly resolved that, out of respect for the past, no change in the structure would be permitted.

We can scarcely realize how intense and compelling was the spiritual power of holy relics in earlier times, for our interest in them today is almost entirely an aesthetic one. Similarly, the figure personifying Justice, standing over the balconied window of the Ducal Palace, divested as it now is of the associations it had for the old Venetians, means no more to us than any other piece of sculpture by Alessandro Vittoria. Things were very different in the past, and if we are not to look upon the Palace as an empty shell and a mere museum, if we are to gain any insight into Venice, her people, her history, her art and civilization, then we must attempt to understand what it was the Venetians of old saw in these walls, these "stones of Venice"; we must, if we can, single out the secret vitality which, beneath the shifting pattern of centuries and styles, gave to the heart and soul of the city, the Ducal Palace, that organic unity, that unmistakable coherence which, whether we realize it at once or not, constitute its abiding fascination.

It is an illusion to suppose that a given period of history can always be understood by focusing one's attention on outstanding events and actions, or anyhow on those held up as such by tradition and literature. For it often happens that the key to a right understanding of the past is supplied not by some heroic figure or conspicuous episode, but by ways of life and thought of which little record remains, the reason being that they were taken so much for granted at the time that they were seldom alluded to by contemporaries.

The Ducal Palace was always regarded by the Venetians as, first and foremost, a precious shrine, the receptacle in which every civic memory and possession was treasured up; and not only real and material wealth, not only objects and documents of practical utility, but also boundless wealth of a political and moral order on which perhaps, in the last analysis, were founded the strength and stability of the state. Here was all whose price, rarity and beauty contributed to enhance the prestige of Venice. Already in the earliest times Venetians boasted of their city as a jewelled shrine. The *Cronaca Altinate* speaks of it as "abounding in all things." "Full of riches and rich in men," sang Guglielmo di Puglia. Martino da Canal, writing in the second half of the twelfth century, described the city as "the most beautiful and most agreeable of the age, full of graces and wealth; goods flow through that noble city like the waters of a fountain." "Speak of luxurious houses and abundance of wares!" exclaimed Georges Lengheraud. "I have been in Paris, Bruges and Ghent, but they are as nothing compared with Venice."

It was of course in the Ducal Palace that the best and greatest of this wealth was enshrined. But before it ever came to house precious manuscripts and classical sculpture presented to the State, before its halls were gilded and decorated, in the deepest, most heavily defended recess of the Palace, near the tower that stood beside the Ponte della Paglia, the "civil treasure" of the Venetians was created and jealously guarded: the Armoury. These rooms, out of fidelity perhaps to ancestral traditions, always continued to inspire a peculiar respect, just as in early days when, in time of danger, they supplied the Venetians with the weapons required to defend the castle against attack. The first museum director was the keeper of the Armoury. To visit these rooms, however, it was necessary to obtain a special permit from the Great Council, a permit issued only after due deliberation. The same procedure was required to visit another place sacred to the Venetians: the Treasure of St Mark's.

JACOPO BELLINI (C. 1400-C. 1471): A VENETIAN PALACE (WITH "THE SCOURGING OF CHRIST").
PEN AND INK DRAWING ON VELLUM. PAGE 29 OF BELLINI'S SKETCH BOOK IN THE LOUVRE, PARIS.

JACOPO BELLINI (C. 1400-C. 1471): VENETIAN PALACE WITH A GOTHIC BALCONY. PEN AND INK DRAWING ON VELLUM.
PAGE 46 OF BELLINI'S SKETCH BOOK IN THE LOUVRE, PARIS.

The stout wooden doors of the Armoury—made, as we have seen, of cedar of Lebanon—gave access to what was nothing less than a complete arsenal, containing not only lances, swords, shields, crossbows and all the weapons of medieval warfare, but also arms and equipment belonging to Doges and famous men (like the suit of armour of Enrico Dandolo brought from Constantinople by Gentile Bellini in 1480, and the armour of Henry IV, Agostino Barbarigo and the Gattamelata), records and precious mementoes (like the portraits of the Carraresi and the illuminated codex containing the genealogy of that family), standards captured from the enemy and such trophies as could not be embodied as ornaments in the external walls or in what Otto Demus has called the "political façade" of St Mark's. In the Armoury, then, we have the oldest civil museum in Venice, the earliest recorded mention of it dating to 1317. The objects preserved in it required no explanation; they spoke the language of political propaganda readily understandable to the men of that time.

There were other treasures in the Palace which served a practical purpose: imperial bulls conferring privileges and tax exemptions issued by foreign cities and governments; proclamations of indulgences granted in 1362 by Pope Urban V (whereby the small church of San Nicolò di Palazzo became a place of pilgrimage); the scale model by Vettor Fausto of a war galley with four banks of oars and mounting three hundred cannons; the reports submitted by Venetian ambassadors abroad (giving fully detailed accounts of the commercial and political situation in each country) and the maps preserved in the so-called Secret Archives. These maps and charts, giving as complete a picture as possible of countries and continents, were kept carefully up to date, being rectified and filled out as new lands were discovered and opened to trade. Indicated on them were "the seaways opened up in our times" and "the shores discovered by the Portuguese"; channels leading into safe harbours were carefully charted, as were the mountain passes by which incursions into enemy territory could be made in case of need, complete with explanatory detail indicating whether the route was passable on horseback or only on foot (Lorenzi).

On the occasion of great receptions and entertainments, the halls and galleries of the Palace contained in profusion the finest products of local manufacture, a dazzling exhibition of the treasures and skills of Venetian industry and craftsmanship. As time passed, though the old ways by no means lapsed and these objects and furnishings retained their prominence as a matter of policy, increasing importance began to be given to plastic and pictorial decorations. Their propaganda value was real and effective, even though indirect, and they aroused the admiration and envy of other nations. The walls and ceilings of the Ducal Palace thus came to illustrate the long, eventful saga of Venetian history. Boschini called it "a heroic picture poem" in which "the most famous painters sing the praises of the most glorious exploits," in order to kindle the patriotic ardour of all who should see them, "that they too, in emulation of these distinguished heroes, may the more zealously strive to leave an honoured memory of their

ANTONIO RIZZO (C. 1440-C. 1499): THE GIANTS' STAIRCASE (1485-1521), SEEN FROM THE ARCO FOSCARI.
THE TWO GIANTS, MARS AND NEPTUNE, WERE ADDED IN 1566 BY JACOPO SANSOVINO.

deeds to generations yet to be born in this Most Serene Republic." "It is fitting," writes Casoni, "that a work should be admirable, not for any fleeting pleasure it may procure, but for the useful results it should produce, and this should be the end and aim of every artist who aspires to praise and esteem, for 'unless what we do is useful our glory is vain.'"

The government appointed committees to choose the official painter and to decide on the themes and sequence of pictures; it saw to it, furthermore, that timely measures were taken to preserve the artistic and moral heritage which these paintings constituted. In the Hall of the Great Council, under the *Paradise* of Guariento, were inscribed some lines from Dante; under the oldest decorations were some inscriptions dictated by Petrarch. How much store the Venetian government set by artists and men of letters is shown by a painting preserved in the Senate Hall, in which the Doge and members of the government are represented extending their protection to historians and poets.

In the employ of the State were not only an official historian, a government architect and a keeper of the Armoury, but also an official painter, who was assisted and advised in his work by iconographic experts, such as Daniele Barbaro, Francesco Sansovino and Gerolamo Bardi. The last-named, in an "Explanation of all the Histories contained in the Pictures lately placed in the Halls..." (Venice, 1585), written to explain the decorations executed in the Hall of the Great Council and the Hall of the Scrutineers after the great fire of 1577, gives a clear account of the criteria adopted in the new decorations of the Ducal Palace: "...in order that everyone may fully understand all that is contained in each public picture." The same need for clarity was felt by Marin Sanudo who, in describing a picture by Titian, at one point imagines the figures themselves as stating the reason for their presence. St Justina, for example, represented in a painting commemorating a Venetian victory over Padua, is made to say that she is present in the picture because it was on her name day that the victory was won. In addition to paintings inspired by the early vicissitudes and civil history of the city, and those which Boschini called "martial histories," there were works of a sacred and devotional character and others on allegorical and mythological themes; numerous, too, were the Apotheoses, particularly in the sixteenth century, in the time of Veronese's *Triumph of Venice*.

Taken as a whole, the paintings in the Ducal Palace fall into two categories: the first includes those of general significance, located in corridors and anterooms; the second, bound up more particularly with Venetian concerns, consists of works addressed to specific persons and groups in authority, to the members of a particular council or office of state. In the latter case they are designed to warn the magistrates against the vices to which, holding the office they do, they might naturally be prone, and to encourage them to cultivate the virtues most suitable to their functions. In the Hall of the Council of Ten, for example, the divinities and allegories on the ceiling illustrate

ALESSANDRO VITTORIA (1524-1608) AND BATTISTA FRANCO (C. 1498-1561):
THE GOLDEN STAIRCASE (1555-1559) LEADING TO THE COUNCIL CHAMBERS IN THE DUCAL PALACE.

ANTONIO RIZZO (C. 1440-C. 1499): PHILOSOPHER.
MARBLE BAS-RELIEF ON THE NORTH SIDE OF THE GIANTS' STAIRCASE.

the powers of the earthly tribunal which, in the image of its heavenly counterpart, punishes crime, sets the innocent free, defends the state on land and sea, encourages trade and science, and contributes to extend Venetian rule. The same principle is applied in the main hall of the Zecca (mint), which is decorated with paintings which, in order to bring home the prestige that derives from wealth, represent the Magi offering their gifts to the Christ-child and the Queen of Sheba amidst her fabulous treasures. Danese Cattaneo, who was both a poet and a sculptor, designed the statues of Apollo, Luna and Venus, symbolizing gold, silver and copper respectively—the metals, that is, required by the mint.

Sometimes, particularly in the Humanist period, painting and marble became the medium for abstruse and scholarly themes; such is the case with the works decorating the Giants' Staircase and the private apartments of the Doge. Sometimes, on the other hand, proverbs and popular notions were illustrated; an instance of this is recorded by Sanudo in his diary. In 1497, meeting Sanudo in the Senate Hall, the Procurator Ferigo Corner said to him: "Marin, my son, do you see how this room has been painted? Do you see those trees, tall, medium and short? They symbolize the persons who come to form part of this Senate. The small must learn by experience, then they attain to middle age, and finally become elders. The three ages are all present in the Senate, with the characteristics appropriate to each: the ardour of youth, the force of maturity, the prudence of old age. By thus blending the three 'bloods,' warm, tepid and cool, and balancing different temperaments, a good amalgam is obtained by which well-designed republics are governed."

The scenes represented had always to be in keeping with the dignity and splendour of the Palace. Thus when Filippo Zaniberti, in a painting in the Banquet Hall, so far forgot himself as to add a playful touch to the picture, in the shape of a little boy trying to fish his dog out of the canal, many protested at this as casting a slur on the dignity of the premises and the solemnity of the theme treated in the painting; and boy and dog had to be painted out.

While the pride of the Venetian citizen was flattered by the trophies, relics and privileges obtained in such profusion by his ancestors, and while he learned to admire their virtues and exploits as represented in painting, there were still other works of art which also urged him to emulate the great Venetians of the past, in hopes of being immortalized, like them, in portraits on the walls of the Ducal Palace. It is true that the Republic set up stone tablets to perpetuate the infamy of evil-doers, that it attached the highest importance to capital punishment as a means of deterring potential criminals, that over the portrait of a Doge who turned traitor it hung the black veil of infamy with the inscription, *Hic est locus Marini Faletri decapitati pro criminibus* (Here is the place of Marin Faliero, beheaded for his crimes). But at the same time Venice was always ready to give public recognition to those of her citizens who deserved well of their country. Thus it was that personages of all ranks and periods, who had distinguished themselves in the service of their country, were represented—even anachronistically—in the frescoes and canvases decorating the Hall of the Great Council.

All the saints to whom the Venetians had a special devotion were represented in St Mark's. Similarly, the Ducal Palace became in time nothing less than a Pantheon

ANTONIO RIZZO (C. 1440-C. 1499): EVE. MARBLE. DOGE'S APARTMENTS, DUCAL PALACE.

of the State, where all citizens who had enhanced the glory and prestige of Venice were fittingly honoured, first of all the Doges. Their effigy figured on coins struck during their period of office, on the Ducal Promise to which they swore upon their election, and on other official documents. The Doge, moreover, had the right to exhibit his portrait in the Hall of the Great Council and in his private apartments in the Palace. In the Hall of the Collegio (the Cabinet) and in that of the Pregadi (the Senate Hall) he was allowed to hang the votive picture representing him beside his patron saints. In St Mark's, in the Hall of the Escutcheon and on the Bucentaur figured the armorial bearings of the Doge's family.

The laws of Venice, with a view to preventing any abuse of power on the Doge's part, stipulated that he should be portrayed *flexis genibus* (kneeling, that is, before the lion of St Mark) and forbade his portrait to be exhibited outside the Ducal Palace in his lifetime. They left him free, however, to arrange for a funeral monument as splendid and self-glorifying as he cared to make it. There seemed no harm in this, and indeed the justification for it is well stated in the will of a Doge who had set aside a large sum for a particularly impressive tomb: "This I do that it may inspire our posterity to endeavour, by the paths of virtue, to attain to the highest ranks of our country."

Titles and privileges, relics and trophies, myths and legends, celebrations and ceremonies, glorification of the State and its political and military achievements, public display of the portraits of famous men, demonstrations of power, and respect for the past— these were the outward expressions of the pride and might of Venice.

But while the lustre of the Venetian name, and the myth created by her commercial abilities and her diplomacy, by her political and economic prestige, while all this has receded into the shadowy distances of history, much of it indeed largely forgotten, the works of her artists are more alive and exert a deeper fascination than ever. They are the life and soul of Venice and the pledge of her immortality.

On the north side of the courtyard of the Ducal Palace, abutting on the transept of St Mark's, is a monument known as the Arco Foscari. Here was represented the Doge kneeling before the Lion of St Mark. Above, on each of the pinnacles, figures a statue personifying one of the virtues necessary for good government. Every detail here was intended to exalt and glorify the State. Rizzo's statues of Adam and Eve were designed for the niches on the Arco Foscari facing the Giants' Staircase: there, where the Doges of Venice were crowned, they symbolized humanity at large witnessing the ceremony. Rizzo, a friend of Antonello da Messina, was steeped in the culture of the Humanists. Thanks to this artist, and to his *Eve* in particular, which is his masterpiece, Venetian sculpture deserves to rank among the leading schools of Quattrocento sculpture.

VENETIAN ART OF THE THIRTEENTH CENTURY: THE DISCOVERY OF THE RELICS OF ST MARK, DETAIL.
WALL MOSAIC IN THE SOUTH TRANSEPT OF ST MARK'S.

4

THE FLOWERING OF THE ARTS

The early history of Venice is marked by an act of rebellion which, in addition to its political importance, has a direct bearing on the history of the arts. In the year 726 the Byzantine Emperor Leo the Isaurian issued an edict forbidding the use of images in Christian churches throughout his dominions. Thus began the period of Iconoclasm, which aroused violent opposition. In the name of their faith, the Venetians rebelled against the authority of Byzantium and asserted their independence. But in showing their determination to keep to the religion of their forefathers, they may well have been prompted, in part at least, by considerations of a practical order. The Venetians, having fallen heir to the markets of the Copts and taken over their flourishing industry of cult images, found here one reason more to stand out against the imperial edict, and threats and anathemas failed to move them. Always quick to take advantage of a favourable opportunity, the Venetians had chosen a good moment to assert their independence: a quarter of a century later, in 751, the Exarch of Ravenna died, the last representative of Byzantine power in Italy.

From 726 on, then, Venice was to all intents and purposes free, though still nominally a part of the Byzantine Empire. In the following century her independence was recognized, first by the pact of Aachen (814), then by the Carolingian Emperor Lothair (840). In the interval between these two dates—in the year 828 according to tradition—the relics of St Mark the Evangelist were transferred from Alexandria to Venice, an event which marks the close of the long period of the city's obscure beginnings.

From the artistic point of view, however, it was not until many years later that Venice achieved any particular distinction. Between 976 and 1000 the first Pala d'Oro, now the great altarpiece of St Mark's, was brought to Venice from Constantinople. Between 1063 and 1071, under the Doges Domenico Contarini and Domenico Selvo, the Church of St Mark's was built, not to any original or contemporary design, but in imitation of a church erected in Constantinople five centuries earlier.

TOMB OF THE DOGESSE FELICITA FALIER, WIFE OF DOGE VITALE MICHIEL. IIOI. WEST ATRIUM OF ST MARK'S.

Meanwhile carved and dressed stones of the most varied origin were being accumulated in the islands of the Lagoon. The early city might be likened to a museum where random objects of every kind, with little connection between them, were gathered together. The tomb of Doge Vitale Falier (1084-1096) and that of the Dogesse Felicita Michiel (1101) in the atrium of St Mark's are composed of heterogeneous elements (pilasters from a small iconostasis, polychrome marbles carved with all the delicacy of fine embroideries, etc.) re-employed with little concern for the unity of vision which alone would have given them life and coherence. But the passage of a few decades brings us to the threshold of the period which saw some of Venice's first artistic achievements.

Before dealing with these, it may be well to survey the events of this period in which Venice was consolidating her political and commercial power. It was in 1095 that for the first time the Doge, as head of the government, assumed the title of Serenissimus— "Most Serene"—in recognition of the peaceful policy he had steadily pursued. In 1117 the growth of trade led to the appointment of consuls to represent the government abroad and protect the interests of Venetians established in foreign parts. An inscription of 1130 on the tomb of Doge Domenico Michiel reads like a challenge to Byzantium. In 1152 we hear of the export of Venetian products to France and the widespread demand for them there, where Abbot Suger of Saint-Denis already possessed a cross *"de façon de Venise."* By 1155 the Arsenal was built, with its great shipyards, "whence issued the mighty vessels innumerable that for centuries maintained the naval supremacy of Venice." In 1156 the image of St Mark appeared for the first time on Venetian coins. In 1167 we hear of the "Venetian law" of the sea being recognized and respected by other nations. In 1172 the Great Council was created, together with other fundamental organs of the Venetian government. Henceforward the Doge represented an able and enlightened oligarchy which was to govern Venice uninterruptedly down to the fall of the Republic six hundred years later. In 1173 the office of a special magistrate was definitely instituted: a kind of supervisor and co-ordinator of the arts. It was in the 1170s, too, that the famous ceremony of the *Sposalizio del Mar,* the Wedding of the Sea, was held for the first time; henceforth, every year on Ascension Day, the Doge, from his State barge, the Bucentaur, dropped a consecrated ring into the sea and declared that Venice and the sea were indissolubly one. Between 1172 and 1178 Doge Sebastiano Ziani renovated and embellished the Ducal Palace, completed the construction of the Campanile in St Mark's Square and the Rialto Bridge, and "had buildings put up round the Square," as an old chronicle relates, "with columns and arcades, after the manner of a theatre, and a corridor running round it, which made it a fine sight to see." It was only with Doge Ziani, in our opinion, that Venice began to sponsor an art of her own.

Now the architecture of the city began to follow definite lines and assume a characteristic style, now its laws began to take definite form. At the same time an art

VENETIAN ART OF THE SECOND HALF OF THE TWELFTH CENTURY: FIGURE PERSONIFYING A CRAFT.
ON THE BASE OF THE COLUMN OF ST THEODORE IN THE PIAZZETTA.

distinctive of Venice made its appearance in sculpture, notably in the representations of the Crafts carved on the bases of the columns in the Piazzetta (about 1175). After the humble, anonymous work of earlier times, these come as the first genuine affirmation of artistic power and originality. Skilfully wrought in huge blocks of stone, these carvings reveal features that we should hardly have expected to find outside France at this time. They have nothing of the rigid abstractionism of Byzantine work or the ponderous inertness of Romanesque decorations (two remarkable exceptions, however, being the splendid Romanesque protomes supporting the arcades inside St Mark's and the sleeping Apostles in the great mosaic of *Christ in the Garden of Olives*). Already the figures personifying the Crafts point the way to the great Venetian sculpture of the thirteenth century.

VENETIAN ART OF THE SECOND HALF OF THE THIRTEENTH CENTURY: FISHERMEN. MARBLE.
DETAIL OF THE CARVINGS ON THE CENTRAL DOORWAY OF ST MARK'S.

The rise of this new art cannot be fully understood without considering the part played by Venice in the Crusades. Already in August 1099 Giovanni Michiel, son of the Doge Vitale Michiel, had supplied Godfrey de Bouillon, one of the leaders of the First Crusade, with two hundred ships. But Venice threw herself into the Fourth Crusade (1203) with all her might. France, more than any other country, was the soul of the Crusades, and the French language accordingly spread and found currency among all the different peoples taking part in them, so much so that the use of Latin was increasingly relegated to official documents and church ceremonies. This was the period in which Provençal poetry spread beyond the frontiers of France, inspired the Sicilian School at the court of Frederick II, gave rise in Germany to the lyrical poetry of the Minnesingers, and thereby opened the way to the coming autonomy of national speech in the modern states soon to be founded in every part of Europe. Among the earliest names in Italian literature we find, in Venetia as it so happens, those of poets writing in Provençal and, a little later, in "Franco-Venetian."

It is important to note the diffusion of French coinage and the presence at Grado as early as the ninth century (803-826) of master builders and goldsmiths summoned from France. But most significant of all for us is the fact that Martino da Canal, between 1267 and 1275, wrote the first history of Venice in French: *La Cronique des Veniciens*. To the same period dates the mosaic in St Mark's representing the *Discovery of the Relics of St Mark*: "This," wrote Bettini, "is one of the outstanding masterpieces of Venetian art."

Also to the 1260s belong the *St Helen* and the other frescoes in San Zan Degolà (i.e., San Giovanni Decollato). Comparing them with the mosaic just mentioned, we notice many similarities in the figures, in the handling of volumes, and in the monumental dignity of the whole conception. But while the frescoes seem to be the end result and final expression of a highly refined civilization, the figures in the mosaic come vividly to life. They are represented in a definite and easily recognizable setting: the interior of the church of St Mark's itself, as it then was. They are shown, furthermore, participating in an episode that unfolds in two successive sequences: first the Doge and people praying for their recovery, then the miraculous appearance of the lost relics. Thus the artist shows himself equally alive to the time factor, whose logic he carefully observes.

"Quant l'en voit painte une histoire, ou l'en oit conter une bataille... nos somes present ou les batailles sont faites" (When we see a story painted or hear the account of a battle, we are present where the battles were fought), wrote Martino da Canal in his *Cronique*, giving already an intimation of the precision and the earthbound immediacy that were to characterize the Venetian aesthetic. The garments, faces and grouping of the different figures in the *Discovery of the Relics of St Mark* have these very qualities; they bring home to us the historic character of the event represented, and

VENETIAN ART OF THE THIRTEENTH CENTURY: THE DOGE AND PEOPLE OF VENICE PRAYING FOR THE RECOVERY OF THE RELICS OF ST MARK.
WALL MOSAIC IN THE SOUTH TRANSEPT OF ST MARK'S.

ST HELEN SHOWING THE WOOD OF THE TRUE CROSS TO THE PEOPLE FROM THE BALCONY OF HER PALACE. THIRTEENTH CENTURY. FRESCO IN THE APSE OF THE CHURCH OF SAN GIOVANNI DECOLLATO.

its importance in the life of the nation. There is nothing mystical or fabulous about this pictorial narrative; nothing abstract, nor, on the contrary, is anything too analytically delineated.

The process of humanization proceeded with the dignity and solemnity of idiom appropriate to history. But, though the Venetians tended to handle themes freely and in an independent spirit, the fascination of the Byzantine world was still strong and always took effect whenever they sought to enhance the "official" prestige of their works. So it was that Paolo Veneziano, founder of the Venetian school of painting, reverted in several of his works to Byzantinizing modes and stylizations. So it was, too, that pictures on a gold ground continued to be painted for so long in Venice, and not only by the Vivarini and Crivelli; as late as the eighteenth century, in pictures by Tiepolo and Guardi, gold backgrounds are still occasionally to be found.

In close contact with Byzantium from the very beginning, and borrowing freely from Byzantine art, Venice was in a position to supply all Europe not only with original products of her own, but with fine imitations of Byzantine enamels and textiles, particularly in the twelfth and thirteenth centuries when such Eastern works became

PAOLO VENEZIANO AND HIS SONS LUCA AND GIOVANNI: EPISODE IN THE LIFE OF ST MARK.
PANEL OF A POLYPTYCH DATED 1345. MUSEO DI SAN MARCO.

JACOBELLO DALLE MASEGNE (ACTIVE 1393-1409): DOGE ANTONIO VENIER (1382-1400). MARBLE. MUSEO CORRER.

fashionable in Western Europe. But the practical-minded Venetians, trained in the hard school of commerce to take a shrewd, straightforward view of things, swayed only by concrete considerations, set little store by the abstract, metaphysical elements that were all important in Byzantine art. These elements they gradually lost sight of. They placed their confidence in man, in his capacities of invention and workmanship. So that while the patron saints shine resplendently amid the gold of the mosaics inside St Mark's, and while the glorious episodes of the history of the Republic are illustrated in the halls of the Ducal Palace, it comes as no surprise to find on the exterior of the church and the Palace, on doors and capitals, and on the bases of the columns in the Piazzetta, a whole series of scenes showing craftsmen at work.

The *Fishermen* carved on the inner side of the arch over the main door of St Mark's is an outstanding example of a particular aspect of Venetian art. Even more remarkable than the searching realism of the delineation are the mastery and the pictorial sensibility with which the medieval sculptor has characterized the fish swimming about in the transparent depths of the water.

Among the legendary founders of the city recorded in the *Cronaca Altinate* is a family of painters named Damarzi. But it is to sculpture that we must look for the earliest surviving evidence of Venetian art. "It is here," as Professor Grabar has written, "that we are farthest removed from Byzantium. The domain of sculpture is the one in which the Byzantine contribution was smallest." As these works show, the vitality of Gothic art was by now sufficient, in most cases, to overcome and stifle the Byzantine tradition. Having to choose between Byzantine hieraticism and Gothic vitality, sculptors like Jacobello and Pier Paolo Dalle Masegne opted for the latter, working in the spirit that was henceforth to inform all Venetian art.

The great buildings erected in the course of the fourteenth century, the mosaics of this period in St Mark's (Baptistery and Chapel of Sant'Isidoro), the frescoes by Guariento in the Hall of the Great Council in the Ducal Palace, and indeed all the arts of Venice, were by this time speaking the language of the West. When it became necessary to transform and enlarge the Ducal Palace, the best architects and sculptors of the day were called in, as is obvious from the quality of the work, for unfortunately their names are unrecorded. And their work reveals the same change in the source of inspiration: it grows increasingly closer to the style then prevailing in Europe and particularly in Italy itself.

This fine marble statue represents the Doge wearing the horned cap of his office. In its original form it showed him holding the standard of St Mark and kneeling before the lion symbolizing the Evangelist. Jacobello Dalle Masegne and his brother Pier Paolo were also responsible for the iconostasis in the church of St Mark's (see page 34). "Both sculptors were exponents of a naturalistic Gothic style which was of great importance in the history of Italian sculpture" (John Pope-Hennessy).

VENICE AND THE RENAISSANCE

"Venice, at the height of her power in the first half of the fourteenth century, had not extended her own metropolitan territory beyond the limits of the Lagoon," writes Luzzato. "All beyond the grass-covered shoals and the marshes dividing the Lagoon from the mainland was foreign territory. Mestre itself, which today is united with Venice, did not then belong to her." Venice seems never to have had any designs on the mainland region at the head of the Adriatic as long as its markets remained open to Venetian commerce. But when about the middle of the fourteenth century Milan, Verona and Padua sought to gain control of the whole region, Venice saw that she ran the risk of being encircled and cut off from her continental markets and overland trade routes. Drawing on her wealth, she engaged the services of the ablest *condottieri* available and, in addition to her naval power, raised a strong land army. In three years' time she had extended her rule as far as the Mincio and Lake Garda. This rapid conquest marks a decisive turning point in the history of Venice; after the Peace of Turin (1381) she was faced with an entirely new set of problems.

"The Lion of St Mark for the first time planted its paw on the mainland," writes Coletti. "This century saw the change, affecting all Venetian life, from an insular to a continental outlook. We shall see the repercussions of this great event which shaped the destiny of Venice, heralding the splendours of the fifteenth and sixteenth centuries and also sowing the seeds of her inevitable decay: all this came of turning to the continent, of abandoning her maritime positions for positions on the mainland."

In 1423 Doge Tommaso Mocenigo spoke out against the policy of expansion, from which we may infer that Venice had successfully carved out for herself in Northern Italy that continental empire of which the Visconti and Sforza of Milan, the Carraresi of Padua and the Scaligeri of Verona had hitherto dreamed in vain. The wise old Doge urged the Venetian Senate to call a halt, to avoid continental entanglements, and warned them against the bellicose policy of Francesco Foscari. But when Mocenigo died shortly afterwards, Foscari was elected Doge and governed the Republic from 1423 to 1457. He made Venice a continental power, one capable of frustrating the ambitious designs of foreign princes on Italy, and one at the same time whose own interests lay in maintaining a balance between the rival city states into which Italy was divided. The sphere of its ruling interests and its actions was now no longer the "known and unknown worlds," as it had been in the days of Marco Polo. In order to hold their own, the Venetians had to narrow their horizon somewhat; renouncing many of their contacts with the rest of Europe, they entered into increasingly close relations with the other regions of Italy, not only politically and economically, but intellectually and culturally as well.

JACOBELLO DEL FIORE (?-1439): THE CORONATION OF THE VIRGIN IN PARADISE. 1438.
PANEL PAINTING ON A GOLD GROUND. GALLERIE DELL'ACCADEMIA.

This changing background goes far to explain the trend of Venetian art which, hitherto Orientalizing and Gothic, now grew increasingly Italian. In token of a certain Florentine influence we find, on the capital of the Ducal Palace illustrating some lines from Dante, the signature of two Florentine masters: *"Duo sotii florentini."* If they did not give their names, the reason is that there was—and always remained—in Venice a strong prejudice against outside competition and the guilds were naturally hostile to foreign artists. So that even as the new trend made headway the established tradition persisted and Venetian art by no means repudiated the florid Gothic that had changed the face of the city, creating the Venice we know today, so richly ornamented with delicate carvings and many-tinted stones, the Venice whose high and shining palaces were described by Philippe de Commynes, ambassador of the King of France, on his entry into the city in 1495.

"I was taken," he writes, "along the main street, which they call the Grand Canal, and it is very broad. Galleys cross it, and I have seen there ships of four hundred tons or more near the houses: and it is the fairest street I believe that may be in the whole world, with the best of houses, and it goes the whole length of the city. The houses are exceedingly large and high, and of good stone, and the ancient ones all painted. The others built within this last hundred years are all faced with white stone brought from Istria, a hundred miles away, and yet have many a large piece of porphyry and serpentine on the front... It is the most triumphant city that ever I saw..."

To this late phase of Gothic architecture, which made such lavish use of pinnacles and traceried carvings that translate into Istrian stone the traditional elegance of Venetian wood carvings—to this phase of architecture there corresponded a highly refined type of painting that dazzles the eye with harmonious and exquisite images, complicated polyptychs in which dainty figures stand out against a glowing gold background. Antonio and Bartolomeo Vivarini, Giovanni d'Alemagna, Jacobello del Fiore and Giovanni di Francia designed their panel paintings for these elegant Gothic churches, and they decorated the Palazzo Foscari and the Ca' d'Oro with secular subjects, views and hunting scenes.

In contrast with the solemn, carefully calculated forms of Renaissance architecture elsewhere in Italy (those for example of Michelozzo, who in 1433 accompanied Cosimo de' Medici during his exile in the lagoons), the native genius of Venice, pursuing other paths, produced such masterpieces as the Ca' d'Oro, in which open spaces and polychrome marble inlays harmonize in perfect equilibrium, with all the transparent grace and lightness of a glass palace. "Of all the idioms to be found in the visual arts of the insular Venice of the fifteenth century," writes Coletti, "architecture is precisely the one which bears the deepest impress of originality. Architectonic language achieved the representative synthesis of the practical motives that conditioned Venetian architecture in the gracefulness and lightness of its structures—a language which the

ANTONIO VIVARINI (C. 1415-1476) AND GIOVANNI D'ALEMAGNA (C. 1400-1450): ST SABINA BETWEEN ST JEROME AND ST EGERIUS. ABOVE, ANGEL BETWEEN ST MARGARET AND ST CATHERINE. ALTARPIECE DATED 1443. CHAPEL OF SAN TARASIO, SAN ZACCARIA.

imagination of gifted artists often succeeded in transforming into noble poetic expression, destined later to become the common currency of even the humblest utilitarian constructions."

The waters of the Lagoon, in their cool depths, reflect in suave and strident antinomies the pink and gold façades of the palaces. The tradition of colour inspired by Byzantine and Arab art, and so gloriously embodied in the great mosaics and paintings, found new expression and unlooked-for refinements in Venetian architecture.

IMAGINARY VIEW OF ST MARK'S, THE DUCAL PALACE AND THE PIAZZETTA WITH THE TWO COLUMNS OF
ST MARK AND ST THEODORE. ABOUT 1400. MINIATURE FROM THE BOOK OF MARCO POLO.
MS. BODLEY 264, BODLEIAN LIBRARY, OXFORD.

VENETIAN GOTHIC ART OF THE FIRST HALF OF THE FIFTEENTH CENTURY:
THE CA' D'ORO ON THE GRAND CANAL. FINISHED IN 1434.

But Venice was well aware that elsewhere in Italy, and particularly in Florence, a new age had dawned. With the easy adaptability of the wise merchant, the Republic at once singled out the leading artists of the day and, resolved for the sake of prestige to have nothing but the best, called in Gentile da Fabriano, Pisanello, Paolo Uccello, Andrea del Castagno, Filippo Lippi and Donatello. Most of these men came from Florence, the cultural capital of Italy, where the new art and new aspirations of the

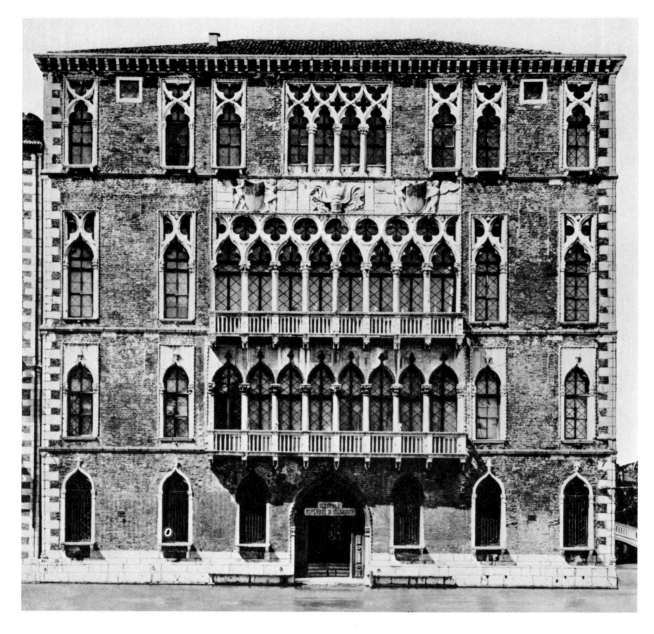

VENETIAN GOTHIC ART OF THE FIFTEENTH CENTURY: THE CA' FOSCARI ON THE GRAND CANAL.

Renaissance had been born. But in the first half of the fifteenth century Florence solicited the political support of Venice, then a power of the first rank, in order to form a common front against the attacks of the Duke of Milan. "For the preservation of our own State and for the liberty of the town of Florence, not only will we gladly help you," replied the Doge to the solicitation of the Florentines, "but we are almost compelled to. For our own preservation and freedom, and Italy's too, we cannot do otherwise than declare war on the Duke of Milan" (Romanin). Florence and Venice thus made common cause: political co-operation was followed by cultural exchanges and Venice prepared herself to take the lead in Italian art. She had learned from the Byzantines and Copts; she had offered asylum to Arab craftsmen; she had welcomed refugees from Lucca who enabled her to establish a monopoly in fine silks; and she had weakened rival cities, depriving them of their privileges and sacred relics, of their patents and markets. Now she sought to place herself in the forefront of the new culture.

While in many fields of endeavour (music, scholarship, the sciences) Venice did indeed make outstanding contributions, thanks to the traditions and intellectual resources of the neighbouring University of Padua, it proved a slow and difficult task for her to assimilate the figurative arts of the Renaissance. The Florentine masters mentioned above, together with Nicolò Lamberti and Nanni di Bartolo, better known as Rosso Fiorentino, were called to Venice, but the work they did there has left little trace and failed to provide the hoped-for stimulation. Even Jacopo Bellini, though he eagerly sought to make himself master of the new vision, failed to enter completely into the spirit of the Renaissance. Not until the end of the century, or more exactly until the first decade of the sixteenth century, with Giorgione, did Venetian painting achieve the happy synthesis and ideal union between instinct and reason, which it had so long aimed at and desired.

UNKNOWN VERONESE ARTIST: A DOGE AND HIS COUNSELLORS. FIRST HALF OF THE FIFTEENTH CENTURY. PEN AND BROWN INK ON PAPER RUBBED WITH RED CHALK. BRITISH MUSEUM, LONDON.

In the meantime far-reaching changes had come about on the political scene. All the cities of Italy had fallen into the hands of princes and powerful lords: it was the age of the despots. Even the ancient republic of Venice could not entirely escape the evils of the century. Between 1485 and 1501 two brothers, Marco and Agostino Barbarigo, succeeded each other as Doge, and there seemed for a while some danger of the establishment of an hereditary dynasty. But the danger was averted in time, the political structure of the state remained unchanged, and Venetians continued to enjoy their ancient liberties.

The scope which the Renaissance gave to the development of individual talents and personality is strikingly exemplified in the *condottieri*, the professional military leaders and soldiers of fortune who sold their services to princes and states at war, and who expected the highest rewards and triumphs in return. Venice, which always chose the commander of the fleet from among her own citizens, made a practice of entrusting the command of her land forces to foreign captains. Scrupulous and thorough as no other Italian city was in training her ablest men as administrators, statesmen and naval officers, Venice prudently abstained from training a body of military leaders in her midst, men inured to violence who, if once they got out of control, might upset the equilibrium of the state and curtail the liberties of its citizens. "The Venetians," wrote Machiavelli, "rather than obey one of their own citizens, avail themselves of the arms of others."

Reverting to the tradition of equestrian monuments prevalent in ancient times, and going for inspiration to the superb bronze horses on the loggia of St Mark's, Venice had statues erected to the memory of its generals: Paolo Savelli (killed in action against the Carraresi in 1405) in the church of the Frari; Erasmo da Narni, the "Gattamelata" (who fought the Visconti and died in 1443), in the Piazza del Santo at Padua; Bartolomeo Colleoni in the Campo dei Santi Giovanni e Paolo (1488) and Leonardo da Prato in San Zanipolo. Another famous statue of a military leader is that of Vittore Cappello on the façade of the church of Sant'Elena. The two great columns in the Piazzetta, moreover, were brought from the East by her fleets and erected as eloquent and premonitory symbols of her striking power by land and sea. It was in the same spirit, with a view to intimidating enemies of the state, that Venice more than any other city so solemnly commemorated many of her generals.

It was in the wars, as a military engineer, that Antonio Rizzo, author of the statue of Vittore Cappello, first distinguished himself. After having "exerted himself in all the batteries and stone-propelling mortars and performed all that was possible in the defence," he returned to Venice where he was appointed Chief Architect of the Ducal Palace, soon establishing himself as the arbiter of the arts in Venice. Breaking with the old traditions of the guilds, he succeeded in bringing highly skilled Lombard craftsmen into Venice. A friend of Antonello da Messina and the Humanists and a

WORKSHOP OF MICHELE GIAMBONO (C. 1400-1462): MEDALLION WITH AN EMPEROR. ABOUT 1430-1450.
DETAIL OF THE MOSAIC REPRESENTING THE DEATH OF THE VIRGIN.
CAPPELLA DEI MASCOLI IN ST MARK'S.

ANDREA DEL VERROCCHIO (1436-1488): EQUESTRIAN MONUMENT OF **BARTOLOMEO** COLLEONI, **DETAIL.** 1481-1488. BRONZE.
CAMPO DEI SANTI GIOVANNI E PAOLO.

ANTONIO RIZZO (C. 1440-C. 1499): MONUMENT OF THE GENERAL VITTORE CAPPELLO, DETAIL. ABOUT 1476. MARBLE.
FAÇADE OF THE CHURCH OF SANT'ELENA.

faithful executor of the plans sponsored by Doge Agostino Barbarigo, he embellished the city with many buildings typifying the style of the Renaissance.

The works of Antonello, the Bellini and other Venetian painters are more helpful to an understanding of Rizzo's art and personality than those of any of his fellow sculptors, whether Venetian or foreign. The initial Gothic rigidity of his work is gradually softened by the intimate plasticism, steeped in northern reminiscences, of the noblest Veronese tradition. Rizzo's handling of marble surfaces, in his hands as malleable as bronze, shows that he had profited by the lessons of Donatello and Pollaiuolo.

The time was at hand when Venice, under the leavening stimulus of all that was most vital in her own early Renaissance, was to rise to the supreme achievements of the sixteenth century. The great name is that of Giorgione, but already clearly discernible in Rizzo's work is the secret of an art such as Giorgione's, an art born of an intimate, soul-stirring experience of the world of the senses.

The work of Mauro Codussi, too, shows traces of Tuscan influence, in particular that of Leon Battista Alberti. He designed the churches of San Michele in Isola and San Zaccaria, the Scuola Grande di San Marco and several palaces on the Grand Canal. His graceful buildings, with pure, clear-cut lines, revive and fuse into a new vision all the artistic experience of the Venetian past. It was no doubt from St Mark's and Byzantine architecture that Codussi derived his fondness for marble facings, the arched silhouettes of his façades reminiscent of the cupolas that were then so numerous in Venice, and the spacious, aerial sweep of his interiors. Light, as it does in Gothic architecture, here floods in through many openings in the thin curtain of the walls, seemingly dematerialized; it thus attenuates the antithesis between external and internal, and the edifice comes to seem a more integral part of the life of the city. His façades are well adapted to the setting in which they stand, enhancing and completing them harmoniously and even festively. Thus the Scuola Grande di San Marco scenically delimits the square in front of the church of Santi Giovanni e Paolo (called in the Venetian dialect San Zanipolo); and the massive nave of the fourteenth-century church is admirably balanced by the high façade of the Scuola beside it. In this desire to harmonize his work with its surroundings and to avoid disproportion or conflict of any kind lie the discipline, the sober distinction, the typically Venetian character of Mauro Codussi's work.

Bartolomeo Colleoni (1400-1475), a soldier of fortune from Bergamo, was appointed captain-general of the Venetian armies in 1455. At his death he left his immense fortune to the Republic, on condition that it should erect a statue to his memory. Verrocchio modelled the monument in clay, his last and greatest work. It was cast in bronze after his death by Alessandro Leopardi and unveiled on March 21, 1496, when—as Marin Sanudo recorded in his Diary—"all went to see it."

ANDREA DEL VERROCCHIO (1436-1488): EQUESTRIAN MONUMENT OF BARTOLOMEO COLLEONI. 1481-1488. BRONZE.
CAMPO DEI SANTI GIOVANNI E PAOLO, VENICE.

ANTONIO RIZZO (C. 1440-C. 1499): MONUMENT OF DOGE NICOLÒ TRON. ABOUT 1476.
IN THE LOWER NICHES, FULL-LENGTH STATUE OF THE DOGE BETWEEN CHARITY AND PRUDENCE. MARBLE. CHOIR OF THE FRARI CHURCH.

PIETRO LOMBARDO (C. 1435-1515): MONUMENT OF DOGE PIETRO MOCENIGO. 1485.
ON THE SARCOPHAGUS, FULL-LENGTH STATUE OF THE DOGE. MARBLE. WEST WALL OF THE NAVE, CHURCH OF SANTI GIOVANNI E PAOLO.

But, as always, it is in painting that the spirit of the city is best revealed—its love of colour, of pageantry, of story-telling, like that in its ancient mosaics, rich in echoes of real life. Gentile Bellini's large painting of the *Procession of the True Cross in St Mark's Square* represents the solemn ceremony, religious and civil at the same time, held annually in the Piazza by the Confraternity of St John. The year is 1496, and in spite of the progress of Renaissance culture in Venice, in spite of the adoption of so many new forms, it is evident from this carefully documented picture that Venice, in her heart and soul, has not changed very much. The Doge and other high

PREPARATORY SKETCH (SOMETIMES ATTRIBUTED TO CARPACCIO) FOR GENTILE BELLINI'S "PROCESSION OF THE TRUE CROSS IN ST MARK'S SQUARE." RED CRAYON SKETCH FINISHED WITH PEN AND INK. BRITISH MUSEUM, LONDON.

GENTILE BELLINI (C. 1429-1507): PROCESSION OF THE TRUE CROSS IN ST MARK'S SQUARE. ▷
DATED 1496. PAINTING ON CANVAS. GALLERIE DELL'ACCADEMIA.

GENTILE BELLINI (C. 1429-1507): DOGE SEBASTIANO ZIANI RECEIVING THE CONSECRATED SWORD FROM POPE ALEXANDER III.
DRAWING IN THE BRITISH MUSEUM, LONDON.

dignitaries of the State figure prominently in this stately ceremony moving from the Porta della Carta round the three sides of the square in front of St Mark's, the whole scene portrayed with marvellous precision. Here is the façade of the church with the original Byzantine mosaics, soon to be destroyed and replaced by new ones; with the as yet unimpaired gilding of crockets, canopies, pinnacles and even the four horses. Here are the old buildings on the right-hand side of the square where the Procuratie Nuove now stand. This is an authentic glimpse of the costumes of early Renaissance Venice, of her grandees, her clergy and officers of state, her leading citizens, parading in order of precedence.

Among those leading citizens was the official painter of the Republic, an office of some importance. It was his duty to look after and safeguard the old paintings, to restore

GENTILE BELLINI (C. 1429-1507): TURKISH JANISSARY. DRAWING IN THE BRITISH MUSEUM, LONDON.

VITTORE CARPACCIO (C. 1465-C. 1525): DOGE SEBASTIANO ZIANI RECEIVING THE STATE UMBRELLA FROM POPE ALEXANDER III IN ANCONA. PEN AND INK DRAWING WITH BISTRE WASHES ON PAPER. E.B. CROCKER ART GALLERY, SACRAMENTO, CALIFORNIA.

and even to repaint them if need be. He designed mosaics, decorations, and the scenery required for ceremonies and feast days in the Ducal Palace and St Mark's. He painted the official portrait of the Doge (which was then copied and set up in all places specified by law), and also his votive picture. The Republic set great store by its artists and made full use of their services, even sending them abroad on occasion. Venetian mosaicists were sent to Rome at the request of Pope Honorius III (1216-1227) to decorate the Basilica of St Paul. Gentile Bellini was sent by the Signory to the court of Sultan Mohammed II in Constantinople, where he was employed from 1479 to 1480. During this time his brother Giovanni took his place in Venice; but on his return Gentile, as the first-born, resumed his official title of *Pittore di Stato*. After Paolo Veneziano, Michele Giambono, Jacobello del Fiore, Gentile da Fabriano, the Bellini and the Vivarini, Carpaccio too was called upon to do some work in the Ducal Palace; like Jacobello del Fiore (1415) and Donato Veneziano (1459) before him, he painted a *Lion of St Mark* (1516) which, like a great banner, still survives in the apartment of the Doges.

In the course of the fourteenth and fifteenth centuries the Ducal Palace was extensively remodelled and "modernized." At the same time a process was repeated that had already occurred once before. As the church of St Mark's with its great domes had begun, centuries before, to dominate the dismal horizons of the Lagoon, all the great families were moved, one after another, to pull down the mean wooden houses of those early days and build for themselves, around the Square of St Mark's and along the canals, fine palaces of stone in keeping with the new dignity and power of the Republic. So now again, as the Ducal Palace was made larger and grander, the whole city was gradually transformed, ennobled, enriched. Wealthy families redecorated their palaces, embellished them with splendid façades. The prosperity of the religious and charitable associations known as Schools *(Scuole)*, which abounded in ancient Venice, was mirrored in their fine buildings and the gorgeous pomp of their ceremonies.

VITTORE CARPACCIO (C. 1465-C. 1525): THE LION OF ST MARK. 1516. PAINTING ON CANVAS.
DOGE'S APARTMENTS, DUCAL PALACE.

All collected who could afford to do so: weapons, coins and curios; relics of the saints; rare and precious objects and antiquities. Such collections increased the prestige both of their individual owners and of the city. In time they grew to vast proportions —the fascinating, infinitely varied units of a store of public wealth, much of which still remains in Venice today as a source of admiration or curiosity.

The passion for collecting was not confined to the fine arts or pious relics. As early as the thirteenth century a Venetian physician named Gualtieri, perhaps in imitation of the Arabs, collected botanical rarities. "A learned curiosity and a sage understanding," we read in a manuscript in the Marcian Library, "prompted our forefathers to admire and know intimately the very plants that supply the most useful products, and the source of much profit for the Venetians. From hence sprang up a boundless passion for growing and nurturing in private homes, with the most lavish expenditure of time and pains, an infinite variety of plants and shrubs from every conceivable region and clime. A learned writer gave it out as his opinion that Venice alone, at one time, may have numbered more private botanical gardens than all Italy does today."

The latent instinct for collecting was increasingly widespread and must have received encouragement from a decree issued by Doge Sebastiano Ziani, according to which (as several of the old authorities report) the Treasure of St Mark's, with its rich collection of relics and reliquaries, provided security for loans incurred by the government. All the old chronicles tell, moreover, how the private fortune of the same Doge was based on the chance find, on one of his estates at Altino, in the ruins of an ancient pagan temple, of a cow of solid gold. The collecting of antiquities, and systematic excavations in search of them, naturally became more widespread with the rise and diffusion of Humanism. "It seemed to me at first sight as if I had entered the Roman Forum when, by the zeal of the Aediles, it was most finely arrayed on days of rejoicing and public games," wrote Paulus Manutius, describing the collection of Andrea Loredan. "I gazed about me, overcome with glad amazement, turning now to the statues, now to the paintings. I seemed to recognize the marble of Praxiteles, the bronze of Polycleitos, the colours of Apelles. Then, approaching the medals, I saw gold and silver. There were many figures there of Greeks and Barbarians, of Romans an infinite number, in fine and well considered order, all portrayed from the life with the utmost verisimilitude, some partly injured by time, some quite entire, even to the eyelashes and the wrinkles of the brow. All the most famous Consuls, all the great Emperors, all the wars, triumphs, arches, sacrifices, costumes and arms stood before my eyes."

When Marco Polo returned from the East in 1295 he brought with him a veritable museum. Some of the objects he collected passed from one family to another, ending in the collection of Doge Marino Faliero and in the Treasure of St Mark's. In 1335 the collection of Oliviero Forzetta contained drawings, sculptures (including nude

GIOVANNI BELLINI (C. 1430-1516): PORTRAIT OF DOGE LEONARDO LOREDAN. ABOUT 1501. PANEL PAINTING.
BY COURTESY OF THE TRUSTEES, NATIONAL GALLERY, LONDON.

figures), candelabra and illuminated manuscripts. Soon after the middle of the same century Petrarch came to live in Venice. His library was rich in newly discovered works of ancient writers, and in an eloquent letter he expressed his intention of bequeathing it to Venice. The long-deferred plan of founding a public library became a reality with the donation of Cardinal Bessarion (March 1468) who, after enjoying the hospitality of the city for twenty years, bequeathed his incomparable collection of Greek manuscripts to Venice rather than Rome, for he felt that of the two it was Venice that formed the most vital link between West and East. Cardinal Bessarion also gave a relic of the True Cross to the Scuola Grande di San Giovanni (the shrine containing it was painted by Gentile Bellini) and generously endowed the Scuola di

VITTORE CARPACCIO (C. 1465-C. 1525): PREPARATORY SKETCH FOR THE PORTRAIT OF CARDINAL BESSARION AS ST AUGUSTINE. DRAWING IN THE BRITISH MUSEUM, LONDON.

VITTORE CARPACCIO (C. 1465-C. 1525): PRESUMED PORTRAIT OF CARDINAL BESSARION AS ST AUGUSTINE, GENERALLY KNOWN AS "ST JEROME IN HIS STUDY." PAINTING ON CANVAS. SCUOLA DI SAN GIORGIO DEGLI SCHIAVONI.

San Giorgio degli Schiavoni (where Carpaccio portrayed him in the dress of a humanist saint intently writing in a room in which a whole collection of objects is displayed).

Artists too were fond of collecting archaeological fragments, copies and casts of famous works, drawings and pictures by other masters. The ostensible reason was to have on hand a varied stock of study material, both for the master and his disciples. But more often than not it was the passion for collecting curious or valuable works that prompted artists to vie even with wealthy collectors like Benedetto Dandolo and Pietro Barbo. The seat of the painters' guild was itself the first museum of Venetian art, for there were preserved the pictures painted, at the age of about eighteen, by each candidate seeking to qualify for the coveted title of "master." Jacobello del Fiore owned an inlaid panel which in 1439 was acquired by Jacopo Bellini; Gentile Bellini owned a Madonna in mosaic, a portrait of Plato and an antique Venus whose praises were sung by the Triestine poet Raffaele Zovenzoni. Andrea Mantegna is known to have had a bust of a Roman empress. All these men were perhaps following the example of Francesco Squarcione of Padua (Mantegna's teacher), who had travelled in Greece and Southern Italy and brought back with him a collection of sculptures, casts and drawings for the use of his many pupils. Andrea Palladio later owned a portrait by Parmigianino, and Alessandro Vittoria had paintings by Titian, Veronese and Bassano, and a foot from Michelangelo's statue personifying Day. In 1535 Aretino brought back to Venice some drawings by Michelangelo; these were studied by Tintoretto, together with other drawings by Giovanni da Bologna and copies of works by Michelangelo made by Daniele da Volterra.

The government regarded works of art as the most fitting gift for foreign princes and dignitaries who were the guests of Venice. In 1534 a Laocoön from the Grimani Collection was presented by the Signory to the Cardinal of Lorraine; later a painting by Veronese was offered to Louis XIV, a St Jerome in mosaic to a Prince of Savoy, and a "cosmography" of Italy to a Cardinal.

Francesco Sansovino, in his *Venetia città nobilissima e singolare*, listed the most interesting private collections in the city. But well before him, in the early years of the sixteenth century, when Marcantonio Michiel began writing a history of Venetian art he explored the city house by house and recorded in his book all that he saw in each. It is astonishing even today to read the accounts of these priceless collections: classical objects, Tuscan bronzes, Flemish paintings by Alberto de Olanda (Ouwater), Rugerio de Burselles (Rogier van der Weyden), Giones de Brugia (Jan van Eyck), Zuan Memelino (Memling), Bosch and many others. Several works by Hieronymus Bosch are still preserved in the Ducal Palace, but nearly all the other paintings of the *maestri ponentini* (i.e., "western masters," as the Flemings were called in Venice to distinguish them from the Byzantine masters) listed by Michiel in the sixteenth century have long since emigrated.

Generally speaking all such works in private hands were eventually sold. Their noble or wealthy owners had no illusions on this score, and those desirous of being remembered by posterity took good care, in their own lifetime, to leave more enduring monuments, founding altars or adding new façades to churches at their own expense. But there was still another means of keeping one's name alive: that of bequeathing notable works of art to the Republic, such as would signally increase the prestige of the State and enrich the national patrimony. Cardinal Zeno presented the Flemish tapestries now in the Museo di San Marco, and the Grimani the famous Breviary still

FLEMISH ART OF THE FIFTEENTH CENTURY: THE EMPEROR SIGISMUND CROWNED BY POPE EUGENE IV, DETAIL.
TAPESTRY OFFERED TO THE REPUBLIC BY CARDINAL ZENO IN 1501. MUSEO DI SAN MARCO.

HIERONYMUS BOSCH (C. 1462-1516): ST JEROME DOING PENANCE IN THE DESERT.
PANEL OF THE ALTARPIECE OF THE HERMITS. DOGE'S APARTMENTS, DUCAL PALACE.

known by their name. The Contarini, the Venier and the Grimani again bequeathed to the State some of the most precious objects in the Archaeological Museum, once housed in the Ducal Palace, but since 1586 in the eminently suitable premises—anticipating those of a modern museum—of the Libreria Vecchia built by Sansovino.

Each donor, in the interests of his own fame, was naturally anxious to secure the services of the leading artist of the day. Hence the statue of Colleoni was entrusted to Verrocchio; the St John in the Chapel of the Florentines in the Frari church to

FLEMISH PAINTING OF THE FIFTEENTH CENTURY: TWO ILLUMINATED PAGES OF THE GRIMANI BREVIARY. MARCIAN LIBRARY.

EL SEQVENTE triũpho nõ meno mirauegliofo dĺ primo. Impo
che egli hauea le q̃tro uolubile rote tutte, & gli radii, & il meditullo defu
fco achate, di cádide uéule uagaméte uaricato. Ne tale certaĩte geftoe re
Pyrrho cũ le noue Mufe & Apolline í medio pulfáte dalla natura ípffo.
  Laxide & la forma del dicto q̃le, el primo, ma le tabelle erão di cyaneo
Saphyro orientale, atomato de fcintillule doro, alla magica gratiffimo,
& longo acceptiffimo a cupidine nella finiftra mano.

Nella tabella dextra mirai exfcalpto una infigne Matróa che
dui oui hauea parturito, in uno cubile regio colloca
ta, di uno mirabile pallacio, Cum obftetrice ftu
pefacte, & multe altre matrone & aftante
Nymphe Degli quali ufciua de
uno una flammula, & delal‑
tro ouo due fpectatiffi
me ftelle.

* *

*

THE TRIUMPH OF PYRRHUS. WOODCUT ILLUSTRATION FOR "THE DREAM OF POLYPHILUS" WRITTEN
BY FRANCESCO COLONNA AND PRINTED BY ALDUS MANUTIUS AT VENICE IN 1499.

Donatello; the altarpiece of the Bon family in San Cassiano to Antonello da Messina; the altarpiece with the Virgin in the Chapel of the German Nation in San Bartolomeo to Dürer. Care was taken to bestow a given commission on the artist or technician whose experience and talents best fitted him for it. Leonardo da Vinci was called in on the strength of his fame as a hydraulic engineer and expert on defensive works. Perugino was invited to contribute to the decoration of the Ducal Palace. The choir of St Mark's was trained and conducted by the most famous Flemish musicians. "It is all to the honour and fame of our city," states a decree of 1403, "that in our church of San Marco good singers are to be heard." Special competitions were held for the post of government architect, for the decorating of Sansovino's Libreria, and for the painting of the *Paradise* in the Hall of the Great Council.

Publishing activities in Venice in the second half of the fifteenth century attracted some of the best printers in Europe, including the guiding genius of this new art, Aldus Manutius, who in 1499 published his masterpiece, the *Hypnerotomachia Polyphili* or *Dream of Polyphilus*, written by Francesco Colonna; the curious encyclopaedic learning of the text is brought vividly to life by the beautiful woodcut illustrations.

MURANO GLASS-WORK OF THE FIFTEENTH CENTURY: ENAMELLED GLASS DISH WITH THE ARMS
OF THE DUCAL FAMILY OF BARBARIGO. MUSEO VETRARIO, MURANO.

In the premises of the Aldine press and in the Academy which Aldus helped to found, as in the villas and houses of Venetian nobles, there gathered the foremost scholars and men of letters of the time, among them Erasmus of Rotterdam. This concourse of active and inquiring minds from all over Europe, with the resulting intellectual ferment and broadened horizons that they brought to Venetian life, provides the background of the period which is, undoubtedly, the Golden Age of Venice.

Only now—and not until now—was Venice able to produce a mature and finished artist: Giovanni Bellini. He was the son of Jacopo Bellini, one of the leading exponents in Venice of the new art; brother-in-law of Andrea Mantegna, the most famous court painter of the day; and younger brother of Gentile Bellini, the artist in whom the government had most confidence. Giovanni was, furthermore, a follower of Antonello da Messina, who first acquainted the Venetians with the revolutionary technique of oil painting invented by the Flemings. He painted frescoes and panels, historical and sacred subjects, portraits and allegories. His spectacular career began with the meticulous linear analysis of International Gothic and the harsh plasticism of Mantegna, and culminated half a century later in a consummate mastery of aerial perspective and tonal painting. And as an old man his vision was still sufficiently keen and fresh for him to appreciate the new beauties of Giorgione's art, and his hand sufficiently flexible to imitate them.

In a letter from Venice (February 7, 1506) Dürer wrote of Giovanni Bellini that, though an old man, he was still the best artist in the city. A fortnight later, on February 23, 1506, Marin Sanudo noted in his diary the death of Gentile Bellini and added: "There remains his brother Giovanni, who is the most excellent painter in Italy." The calm assurance that emanates from his work, the spiritual serenity in which it is steeped, together with the purity of his forms, are like a mirror of the nobility, dignity and serenity of Venice herself.

"In our great and glorious city of Venice are to be found ambassadors of all the powers of the world: of the Pope and the Emperor, of the King of France and the King of Aragon, of the Turkish Sultan and the Duke of Milan, of all the Princes and Signories of Italy, intent on seeing and hearing whatever was determined on by this high and mighty Signory of Venice, protector of Italy and defender of the Church." Thus wrote Girolamo Priuli in 1495. It is not too much to say that Giovanni Bellini, better than anyone else, represents this Venice. He worked for princes and private patrons but—in keeping with the tradition of his family—he considered himself the painter of the State, an artist in the public service. His position was thus defined in an official decree of February 26, 1483. "For his excellent talent in the art of painting Giovanni Bellini is appointed official painter *(Pictor nostri Dominii est appellatus)*. He is charged with the task of restoring the Hall of the Great Council, for which he will be remunerated by our government in order to release him from any other obli-

GIOVANNI BELLINI (C. 1430-1516): FOUR ALLEGORICAL PANELS. ABOUT 1490.
GALLERIE DELL'ACCADEMIA.

gations and enable him to devote himself to this work alone. By authority of the undersigned Councillors of State, Andrea da Molino, Maffeo Contarini, Giovanni de Lege and Frederico Cornaro, in consideration of these his duties, the master Giovanni Bellini is hereby exempted from all dues and obligations to the School or Confraternity of the Painters' Guild. While he is working in the Ducal Palace, those enrolled in the aforesaid School will continue to fulfil all the duties of the Guild and to pay the dues, taxes and expenses of public illumination. All in these presents resolved on shall be communicated to the officials of the Magistracy of Justice, that our ordinances may be duly observed and respected."

It is this official side of his life and personality that chiefly distinguishes Giovanni Bellini from Giorgione, though from the technical point of view he had already mastered all the secrets of the painter's craft. But while Giovanni Bellini had behind him the authority of the State and the traditions of his family and the Painters' Guild, Giorgione appears to be less indebted to the past. He came from the mainland province nearest to Venice and most faithful to it, but at the same time the most independent-minded and adventurous—"the beautiful country of Treviso, with its clear fountains gay," as a Florentine exile, Fazio degli Uberti, wistfully described it. The district around Treviso, still today a countryside of smiling and romantic charm, lay on the main trade route from Venice to Flanders: the road coming down from Germany and the Brenner Pass which, after crossing the Piave Pass in the Venetian Alps, reaches the sea at Venice.

It has been said of Treviso that in its colours and the waterways that wind through the city it resembles Bruges; and the resemblance is borne out by tales of chivalry, a Castle of Love and the stories of Boccaccio. Painters of Flemish origin had settled there, preferring Treviso to Venice, and the city had always played host to musicians and singers of the Low Countries; in 1414 Magister Nicolaus of Liège was cantor of Treviso Cathedral. Cima da Conegliano, a painter as suave as Memling, was the most faithful interpreter of this region. We must not go to him for myths or hieratic expression, but he was gifted as few others were in conveying his joy in the sensuous beauties of nature.

Reproduced on the opposite page are four of a series of five small allegorical panels by Bellini preserved in the Accademia. Each measuring about a foot in height, they were presumably designed to form part of a small piece of furniture once owned by the painter Vincenzo Catena and recorded in his will (April 15, 1530). These fascinating little paintings are full of mysterious allusions and symbols, drawn no doubt from emblem books of the time. They have been explained in various ways. The white-robed lady with a globe (upper left), seated in a boat, may be interpreted as an allegory of Fortune. The female nude holding up a mirror in which a man's face is dimly seen (upper right) is Truth, or perhaps Prudence. The nude man in a large shell (lower left), holding a serpent, is Slander; this panel is signed IOANNES BELLINUS. The fourth panel (lower right) represents the chariot of Bacchus and may be interpreted as an allegory of Sensuality and Virtue.

GIORGIONE (C. 1478-1510): THE TEMPEST. PAINTING ON CANVAS. GALLERIE DELL'ACCADEMIA.

The subject of this picture is a famous legend of St Mark. A fisherman on a stormy night was persuaded by three strangers to row them into the open sea beyond the Lido, where they met a great galley manned by demons approaching Venice with terrific speed, bent on destroying the city. The three strangers, revealing themselves to be St Mark, St George and St Nicholas, exorcised the demons and saved the city. The saints are in the bark on the right: Mark making the sign of the cross, George in knight's armour, Nicholas in his bishop's robes. In their consternation some of the demons are leaping overboard, others are clinging to the rigging and sitting on the masts which flame with fire; still others are in a bark in the foreground, while another bestrides a sea monster. The city of Venice is visible on the horizon.

GIORGIONE (C. 1478-1510) AND OTHERS: ST MARK SAVING VENICE FROM A SHIP OF DEMONS ON A STORMY NIGHT. PAINTING ON CANVAS. SALA DELL'ALBERGO, SCUOLA GRANDE DI SAN MARCO.

In the opulent beauty of the same countryside of Venetia the restless spirit of Lorenzo Lotto found peace for a time, and to the Castle of Asolo, near Treviso, Caterina Cornaro, Queen of Cyprus, retired to console herself for a lost kingdom in the quiet pleasures of a small court and the patronage of art and literature. The Venetian government had assigned her a considerable estate, in itself almost a kingdom in miniature, comprising gentle hills and valleys, splendid buildings and theatres, fairy-like fountains and gardens. The dispossessed queen received a pension of 8,000 ducats a year, but the pomp and display of her court at Asolo, with the visits of princes and lords, and the distraction of entertainments and concerts, could never reconcile her to the bitter memory of having been forced to resign her island kingdom into the hands of the Republic of Venice.

This cultivated court in the hill town of Asolo was only a few miles from Castelfranco, where Giorgione was born in the 1470s. After 1489, the year the queen settled there, her court attracted many young men of the greatest families, who, restless and discontent with the sterner world of their elders, resorted there for music-making, entertainment and good conversation. Here is how Vasari describes Giorgione, who might have been one of those young men. "He delighted continually in the things of the heart and lute music pleased him marvellously. He himself played and sang so divinely that he was often in demand for music-making and celebrations attended by noble persons." While the Republic contended against pressing difficulties, Giorgione was inventing mythological and archaeological landscapes and giving expression to his own immortal dreams of a new Arcadia.

For centuries it had been the settled policy of the Venetian government to prohibit even philosophical and cultural societies from meeting in secret sessions. To understand the *Tempest*, one of Giorgione's most enigmatic paintings, we may perhaps turn to the *Dream of Polyphilus*, written in the late fifteenth century by Francesco Colonna, of Treviso, who belonged to the same circle as Giorgione, for this book is one of the very few sources now remaining from which we can learn at first hand something about that circle. How is it that Marcantonio Michiel, when he saw the painting a few years later (as he saw all the paintings in Giorgione's early manner), failed to grasp its allegorical meaning and merely described the work, on the basis of its representational elements, as "a landscape with a gipsy and a soldier"? What had happened in the meantime to dim the memory of the past? A glance at the stormy course of contemporary events will help us to answer these questions.

In the middle years of the first decade of the sixteenth century Venice found herself hemmed in by enemies. "The Venetians," wrote Machiavelli, "had become so arrogant as to call the King of France the son of St Mark; they had no respect for the Church; and they took it for granted that they would have to set up a monarchy similar to the Roman one." "Occupying all the lands within their reach as occasion offered," wrote Guicciardini, "they openly sought to subdue all Italy." And another writer went even further: "Once they gain control of Italy, it will be easy for them to subjugate all the other nations and found an Empire stretching from East to West." Pope Julius II (1503-1513) accordingly lost no time in arousing "all the Christian princes against them" (Machiavelli).

Venice, resorting in desperation to every diplomatic manœuvre that wisdom or cunning could suggest, sought to elude the dangers threatening her by a system of treaties and alliances. But the time for diplomacy was past. The situation was so critical that in 1506 Jean Lemaire de Belges, while in Venice as secretary to Margaret of Austria, had the impression that the bells of the city were tolling its death knell. "Certain prophecies, oracles and portents there are," he wrote, "which some interpret to mean that the end and doom of the Signory of Venice has come." But Venice held out with unflinching tenacity, drawing on all her strength and accumulated wealth to outface her enemies and stave off impending ruin.

In 1506 the Spaniards occupied some of the key points along the North African coast: the flow of gold that had come to Venice from the Sahara was for a time reduced to a trickle and there was panic and bankruptcy among the merchants on the Rialto. It began to be feared, too, that the discovery of America would prove fatal to Venetian commerce. "Columbus," it was said, "has caused more harm than all the Genoese of old ever did. For by his discovery of the new world he has shown how to bring by sea from East to West those spices and aromatics which, borne on camels' backs to Aleppo and thence by sea to Venice, had made her the emporium of all Europe."

As early as 1504 it had been proposed to by-pass the long ocean route to the "Indies" by digging a canal across the Isthmus of Suez, but the idea was never followed up. In the summer of 1506 news reached Venice of the league formed against her by the Pope and the Emperor Maximilian I. "It produced such a panic in the city," wrote Sanudo in his diary, "that all day on the 25th and 26th of August the utmost disorder prevailed in the flour market, for great numbers of gentlemen, and others besides, bought up the flour as if the enemy were at the gates of Venice already... Even the porters of the storehouses of San Marco bought and hoarded flour... This raised the price by twenty *soldi* a bushel."

Rumours of impending famine and general bankruptcy were rife. The printing offices of Aldus Manutius were closed down (he seems to have issued few if any volumes dated 1506), and the government took drastic steps to check the crisis. Things had come to such a pass that even the young gentlemen-humanists of Giorgione's circle left their country-seats, their life of leisure and revelry, to present themselves at the Ducal Palace and solicit the political and administrative responsibilities to which they were destined by birth, but which hitherto they had shunned.

"Finally came the year 1507..." writes Vasari. The youthful set of returning nobles and humanists brought their painter with them. From this moment the veil of mystery shrouding his youth is lifted and he appears on the stage of history. For the first time he is officially commissioned to do some work in the Ducal Palace (a record of payment is dated August 14, 1507), then in the churches and mansions of the city (on December 11, 1508, he had already finished the frescoes of the Fondaco dei Tedeschi and received payment for them). It is only the works executed from this time on for the public and the city that are recorded by Vasari—works of which no mention is made by Michiel, who lists only the pictures in Giorgione's early manner, apparently quite unknown to Vasari. Between these two accounts, though written at an interval of only a few years from each other, a sharp break appears to intervene, like that dividing two different ages.

"It was like seeing a bright ray of sunlight," said one writer of Giorgione's frescoes on the Grand Canal front of the Fondaco dei Tedeschi, which have now totally disappeared, except for a dim fragment preserved in the Accademia. From all accounts the divinities represented there appear to have scaled the heights of secular painting, a lofty and resplendent work in complete contrast with the hieratic immobility, equally fine in its way, of the Byzantine and medieval mosaics in St Mark's. "Giorgione,"

JACOPO SANSOVINO (1486-1570): THE LOGGETTA AT THE FOOT OF THE CAMPANILE IN ST MARK'S SQUARE. BUILT IN 1537-1549.

wrote the late Lionello Venturi, "combined the three tendencies then predominant in Venetian painting: the reality of life conveyed in plastic relief (Mantegna, Alvise Vivarini, Gentile Bellini); proper respect for religious authority (Giovanni Bellini); and a keen interest in the pageantry of Venetian life (Carpaccio)."

Giorgione's later manner, especially in the Fondaco frescoes, voices the irrepressible spirit of a glorious and triumphant Venice. For while in fact the city was fighting for its life against the League of Cambrai, and not a few had gloomy forebodings of disaster, there were others, especially among the younger men, who never for a moment lost their confidence in the ultimate victory of Venice and their faith in her high destiny. It was the proud confidence and steadfast faith of these younger men that Giorgione's art reflected. He bore witness to the universality of Venice, to the wisdom and efficiency of her institutions (the city of Nuremberg, on June 6, 1506, asked for a copy of some of her laws), the protection of her divinities, and the right that Venice had acquired to consider herself the reincarnation of ancient Rome. The glow of patriotic pride that inspired the Fondaco frescoes rekindled the Venetians' faith in the grandeur of their past and their determination to remain worthy of it.

Unfortunately events took a turn for the worse. Diplomacy and alliances were unavailing, and the united armies of the League of Cambrai pressed to the very shore of the Adriatic. Enemy artillery was set up on the beaches of Mestre. There seemed no hope of checking the invaders or saving anything from imminent disaster. "Unheard of, what no man in the world would have believed, that in less than twenty days the Venetian State should thus come to ruin," wrote Martino Merlini in 1509. In that year, on May 14, Venice lost the battle of Agnadello, which marked the end of her reckless policy of territorial expansion on the Italian mainland. A few months later, in the port of Diu on the Indian Ocean, a naval battle was fought between the Portuguese and the Indo-Egyptian merchants who dealt with the Venetians. The victory of the Portuguese was thought to be a decisive blow at Venetian commercial supremacy and the first step towards breaking up her great network of intercontinental trade routes for the benefit of her competitors.

"Humbled in their pride," the Venetians, who at first seemed "heart-stricken" in their "forlorn and afflicted city," began to examine themselves and consider the causes and effects that had reduced them to such an extremity. The result was a definite and lasting change of policy. Indeed it is not too much to say that seldom in history has a nation known how to stop and draw back at the right moment, as Venice did after the Peace of Bologna (December 23, 1529 - January 5, 1530). "They bethought themselves," wrote the French ambassador, "that for their own good, and in the interest of the State, it were wiser to refrain from involving themselves in war with anyone, but rather to seek and keep the peace with everyone." "The Serenissima," wrote Nani, "turned all its thoughts to the art of self-preservation and peace."

JACOPO SANSOVINO (1486-1570): APOLLO. BRONZE. LOGGETTA, ST MARK'S SQUARE.

VENICE TRIUMPHANT

While "peace" was the watchword galvanizing the efforts of ambassadors and legates, orators and legislators, merchants and scholars, "self-preservation" was the thought uppermost in the minds of all; the prudent Venetians therefore, while suing for peace, neglected nothing that might contribute to the defence of the city, building forts and redoubts and massing artillery at the approaches to the city. Then, after her crushing defeat at Agnadello, just when all seemed lost, by an almost miraculous turn of events the projected invasion of Venice and partition of her mainland holdings failed to take place. The Pope, mistrusting his allies, withdrew his troops; the King of France, having already amassed considerable booty, disbanded his army, while the Emperor marched back over the Alps. Venice, to her relief and amazement, had not only survived the crisis but retained her Italian possessions almost intact. The unequal struggle against the League of Cambrai, however, brought about a change of heart. Her setbacks in the war and her very narrow escape from utter ruin were a sobering experience, one that sank deep into the minds of all and even led to some radical changes in the structure of the State. Now as never before Venice gave thought to questions of home policy: the organization of her bureaucracy, the improvement of her mainland territories, and the appearance of the city itself. For the first time she was free to do so. By renouncing, as she now did, the risks and outlay of many of her more hazardous overseas ventures, she was able to divert the capital thus released into sounder investments at home (industry, building, real estate), which went to make the city more opulent and flourishing than ever.

To begin with, a whole programme of public works was embarked on. By official decree (March 20, 1530) the small shops under the arcades of the Ducal Palace, hired out to vendors of Flanders cloth, were pulled down and swept away. Booths and stalls had, in course of time, sprung up like weeds around the Campanile and the columns in the Piazzetta, blocking the view of the lagoon; these too were now cleared away. Special laws were enacted with a view to protecting and displaying the city's cultural heritage: in 1530 the Treasure of St Mark's was reinstalled in a stately chapel of the church; the collection of antiquities bequeathed by the Grimani was housed in suitable premises

Designed by Jacopo Sansovino, the Loggetta was built between 1537 and 1549. In his *Venetia città Nobilissima et singolare*, the architect's son Francesco Sansovino, the Venetian historian and iconographer, explained the significance of the four bronze statues on the façade. They symbolize the qualities to which Venice owed her long life and prosperity: Pallas Athene alludes to the wisdom of the Venetian government; Mercury, to the power of letters and eloquence; Apollo, god of music, to the harmony that emanates from all the higher spheres of the Republic; the last statue personifies Peace.

in the Ducal Palace. After the death of Pope Leo X (1521) and the disastrous sack of Rome (1527) many artists left the papal court to seek employment elsewhere. Among them was Jacopo Sansovino who, "coming to Venice with the intention of seeking repose for a fortnight," wrote his son Francesco, "there remained forty-seven years and there died."

Sansovino's first patron was Andrea Gritti, one of Venice's greatest Doges, who set him to work repairing and consolidating the domes of St Mark's, which were falling into decay. Thereafter he played a leading part in reconstructing and embellishing the city. He designed the Loggetta alongside the Campanile, also the Libreria Vecchia and the Zecca (i.e., the mint). He widened many of the ancient *calli*, or lanes ("thus raising the rent of the houses and shops to which they gave access," commented Vasari). He replanned and reordered the Rialto district, the old centre of commerce

The beautiful bronze pedestals of the three flagstaffs in front of St Mark's were designed and cast in 1505 by Alessandro Leopardi to replace the old wooden supports, which are clearly visible in Gentile Bellini's picture, dated 1496, of the *Procession of the True Cross in St Mark's Square* (reproduced on page 144).

ALESSANDRO LEOPARDI (C. 1460-C. 1523): BRONZE PEDESTAL IN ST MARK'S SQUARE. 1505. ONE OF THE THREE PEDESTALS OF THE FLAGSTAFFS FROM WHICH THE BANNERS OF THE REPUBLIC FLEW.

ALESSANDRO LEOPARDI (C. 1460–C. 1523): PERSONIFICATION OF ABUNDANCE WITH MERMAIDS AND SEA HORSES.
DETAIL OF A BRONZE PEDESTAL IN ST MARK'S SQUARE. 1505.

and trade. He rebuilt many churches, palaces and public buildings, changing the face of Venice, for from the time of his arrival "nothing was done without his help and counsel."

Vasari, in the sixteenth century, already grasped the "urban" value of Sansovino's architecture which, graceful and scenic, was designed to make the most of pictorial effects, of the play of light and shadow. Open spaces were multiplied, walls enriched and diversified by projections, surfaces broken up with a wealth of decoration. The work of art came to life in perfect harmony with the atmosphere surrounding it. Sansovino, in other words, who was not a Venetian, yet had taste enough, and humility enough, to comply with the unwritten laws that must govern town planning in the unique setting of the Venetian lagoon. His arrival there could not have been better timed, coinciding as it did with the change of outlook that had come over Venice and the fresh concentration of energies on the city itself.

Writers and chroniclers of that period came increasingly to compare Venice with ancient Rome. It may seem surprising that they should have done so at the very time when the Republic was on the defensive. Yet both in Italy and in all Europe, especially after 1530, the "myth" of Venice laid hold of men's imagination and impressed itself on their minds. As her effective power waned, the grandeur of her past loomed larger than ever, and her fame—or, as sixteenth-century writers called it, her "reputation"—grew and spread. Venice came to be looked upon as a model state, admired for her internal constitution and her "free government." "For the sanctity of her laws, the impartiality of her justice and virtue, and in other respects equally deserving of note," wrote Sabellico, "Venetian ways as compared with those of Rome may well be not only in no wise inferior to them, but even better devised." Venice, for her system of government and political "wisdom," henceforth became an indispensable object of study for political thinkers everywhere—Machiavelli among them—and one of the glories of European culture. The sixteenth century passed and so did the seventeenth: all the while the halo of glory clung to the Serenissima, the Serene Republic, and maintained her European "reputation." Her standing among the nations was accordingly far higher than it would have been if proportioned to her effective political power. The renown of her *sanctissime leze*, her "most holy laws," was the moral and cultural heritage which Quattrocento and Cinquecento Venice handed down to later times. Now that she preferred to be accused of cowardice rather than resort to arms, a spontaneous wave of sympathy went out towards Venice and everything Venetian.

"Our state and domains are open and free to Lutherans and heretics, nor can we proscribe them," wrote the Signory in 1530 to the Emperor Charles V. And Sansovino is recorded as saying that Jews living in Venice "thrive there in singular peace, as in a true Promised Land." Taking advantage of the wars that had paralyzed the com-

ALESSANDRO VITTORIA (1524-1608): PORTRAIT OF DOGE NICOLO DA PONTE. ABOUT 1585. TERRACOTTA. MUSEO DEL SEMINARIO.

TITIAN (C. 1488-1576): THE PESARO MADONNA. 1519-1526. ON THE LEFT, BISHOP JACOPO PESARO KNEELING BEFORE ST PETER AND THE VIRGIN. ON THE RIGHT, THE BISHOP'S FAMILY COMMENDED BY ST FRANCIS. SECOND ALTAR, LEFT SIDE OF THE NAVE, CHURCH OF THE FRARI.

mercial life of so many cities in Northern Italy and also their distant rivals in the Low Countries, Venice in the sixteenth century took the lead in wool manufacture and established herself as the foremost industrial centre of Italy. Much of the wealth made available by the curtailment of overseas trading ventures was now invested in property and in land improvement.

Among the reliefs on the bronze pedestals in front of St Mark's, in addition to symbols of Venetian possessions in the East, Alessandro Leopardi represented a satyr presenting Neptune with the richest fruits of the earth. The theme alludes to the products with which Venice was supplied each year by her possessions on the Italian mainland—a large part of which, however, were marshlands. The vast programme of reconstruction and self-improvement undertaken after the Peace of Bologna led the Venetians to take a fresh interest in their mainland territories, an interest motivated too by the desire to prevent the yearly outflow of money required to buy wheat abroad. Alvise Cornaro was the moving spirit in this endeavour to reclaim the fens and waste lands at the head of the Adriatic. It proved entirely successful, creating the new sources of supply and income of which the readjusted political economy of the Republic stood badly in need.

Alongside the rivers channelled into new beds protected by embankments, in the vicinity of the expanding river ports, and on the vast plots of open ground drained and planted amidst the receding marshes, there sprang up the first of the great patrician houses and villas of Venetia, designed by Falconetto, Sansovino, Sammicheli and, above all, Palladio, in emulation, as it might almost seem, of the palatial villas built by the Romans on the shores of the Lagoon and mentioned by the ancient historians. The patricians for whom these villas were built are the men immortalized in the portraits of Titian, Vittoria and other Venetian artists of the sixteenth century. The strength of Venice lay no longer in overseas trade or the supremacy of her arms. Her prestige was henceforth bound up with the ruling class which now, more than ever before, was in a position to enjoy—and display—the fruits of its incomparable social breeding and political experience.

On the first floor of the Ducal Palace is the Avogaria, the office of the Avogadori, the magistrates who kept the famous *Libro d'Oro*, or Golden Book, which was the peerage of the Venetian aristocracy. In the Golden Book were entered the births, deaths and marriages of all the noble families belonging to the patrician class (about two thousand persons all told), which alone could sit in the Great Council. The *Libro d'Argento*, or Silver Book, was the family register of the lesser nobles, or burghers; from this class came those who occupied secretarial and administrative posts in the government. On December 16, 1530, there was published an allegorical poem dedicated to Venice and patterned, in its main lines, on the Divine Comedy. In it the prisons of the Ducal Palace were likened to the Inferno and the State tribunals to Purgatory, while Paradise was compared with the Hall of the Great Council, where the highest earthly assembly, seated beneath the *Paradise* painted by Guariento over the tribune, looked up to it as its sublimest model.

Diplomatists and ambassadors, magistrates and administrators, scholars and historians, churchmen and theologians: generation after generation Venice produced able leaders and men of commanding personality. It was in Venice that the wisest efforts of Catholic reformers were made to counteract the rise of Protestantism by welcoming the stimulus of renewal, and there that the foundations were laid of the Council of Trent. Painting, sculpture and architecture continued to be represented in Venice by men of genius, while Andrea Gabrielli, organist and choir master of St Mark's, and his nephew Giovanni gave a new breadth and richness to Renaissance music.

A vast painting by Marco Vecellio in the Hall of the Council of Ten, in the Ducal Palace, represents the *Peace of Bologna*. It shows Pope Clement VII and the Emperor Charles V discussing the terms of the treaty, while the halberdiers around them make way for an old man of vigorous and imposing aspect: Titian himself, Marco Vecellio's uncle. "Tiziano was sent to Venice as a mere boy of nine to learn to paint in the house of Sebastiano, father of Valerio and Francesco Zuccato, unrivalled masters in the art of mosaic... But afterwards the boy was placed under Gentil Bellino who then, together with his brother, was at work in the Hall of the Great Council. But Tiziano, urged by nature to greater things and seeking perfection in this art, left Gentile and contrived to approach Giovanni Bellino; but neither did the latter's manner wholly satisfy him, and so he chose Giorgio da Castelfranco." Thus, in the words of Dolce, did Titian begin the long and prolific career that was to give to painting a new vitality and power rich in intimations for the future.

"Titian," wrote Cavalcaselle, "although in another form, yet brings to mind the supernatural force of Michelangelo." It was said that the picture he made for the Scuola Grande di San Rocco had wrought miracles. It was only by a miracle too, or so it seemed, that his painting of *The Faith* in the Ducal Palace escaped destruction by fire. His altarpiece with St Peter Martyr was under the special protection of the State and it was forbidden on pain of death to take it out of the city. A halo of majesty surrounded the painter who had allowed an emperor to stoop for the brush that had fallen from his hand. A man of devouring ambition, acquisitive and jealous of his authority, Titian reigned supreme in the Venetian art world for over half a century, imposing on all his will, his tastes, his protégés. Better than any other painter, he conveys the solemn mien and majestic dignity of the Venetian aristocracy in its heyday, taking homage as its due and glorying in its triumphs. Everything he touches acquires a full-blooded life, a dignity and prestige of its own. Even in the works of his extreme old age, there is no sign of faltering; the powers of his maturity, almost superhuman though they seemed, remained unimpaired to the very end.

TITIAN (C. 1488-1576): THE PESARO FAMILY, DETAIL OF THE PESARO MADONNA. 1519-1526. LEFT SIDE OF THE NAVE, CHURCH OF THE FRARI.

TITIAN (C. 1488-1576): HORSEMAN TRAMPLING A FALLEN ENEMY. PREPARATORY SKETCH FOR "THE BATTLE OF CADORE" (DESTROYED IN 1577). GRAPHISCHE SAMMLUNG, MUNICH.

TITIAN (C. 1488-1576): LAMENTATION OVER THE DEAD CHRIST, DETAIL. BEGUN IN 1573, FINISHED BY PALMA GIOVANE.
PAINTING ON CANVAS. GALLERIE DELL'ACCADEMIA.

TITIAN (C. 1488-1576): LAMENTATION OVER THE DEAD CHRIST. BEGUN IN 1573, FINISHED BY PALMA GIOVANE.
PAINTING ON CANVAS. GALLERIE DELL'ACCADEMIA.

One cannot help wondering what the pictures were that the precocious young Titian executed in the studio of Gentile Bellini. And what were those he painted under Giovanni Bellini, before working with Giorgione on the frescoes of the Fondaco dei Tedeschi, "being then barely twenty years old"? In studying the *Old Woman ("Col Tempo")* in the Accademia, now generally attributed to Giorgione, I have been struck by the direct and solid presentment of the figure and by a certain dryness in the handling of it. This searching analysis of reality, the turn of the head on the sturdy neck, the avoidance of immobility by bringing out the dynamism of attitude and speech —all these elements seem to me far removed from the contemplative serenity of Giorgione. I felt that Giorgione would not have been able to break away so completely from the introspective moods that culminate in the enchantment of dreams and the stillness of sleep. I remembered how sharply and analytically some of the figures in Gentile Bellini's large canvases are delineated. I thought of the old peasant woman selling eggs in Titian's *Presentation in the Temple*; though later in date, her heavy hands and expressionistic harshness seemed to me much the same. But the colour of the *"Col Tempo"* picture is definitely that of the opening years of the Cinquecento; so perhaps the critics were right who found the whites here similar to those in Giorgione's *Tempest*.

As I turned these thoughts over in my mind, my attention was arrested by Titian's San Rocco *Christ*, and this painting provided what seems to me now the most plausible solution. The facial expressions of Christ's tormentors (which owe something to Mantegna, Leonardo and Dürer), the sparing application of the pigments, and a certain dryness in the colours suggested a definite connection with the *Old Woman* in the Accademia, and, by pointing to Titian, gradually resolved my doubts. If Dolce's statement is to be trusted, these two works could give me some idea of Titian's way of painting before he overcame problems of form and made his new discoveries in colour. Evidently he had already been impressed by the art of Giorgione, though the flash of revelation, the "little flicker of light," as Dolce called it, had yet to come. The San Rocco *Christ* seems to me essentially pre-Giorgionesque both in the chiaroscuro and the handling of form. Yet in this work, as in others of the same period (the Giustiniani portrait, the Pitti *Concert*), Titian appears to have possessed himself of the spirit of Giorgione. We are not very far here from his discovery of colour, whose first glimmerings can perhaps be detected in the *Three Ages of Man* in the Palazzo Pitti (attributed by some to Giovanni Bellini), in which the shadow of the hair falling over the young man's cheek has a density no other painter could have attained. The figure on the left has an expressive violence again reminiscent of the *Old Woman*, but already endowed with a truthfulness achieved not only by line but by that dense impasto which later led to *The Tribute Money* in Dresden.

A thorough reconsideration of the *Old Woman* in the Accademia, the marvellous San Rocco *Christ* and the *Three Ages of Man* in the Pitti might well justify Dolce's state-

TINTORETTO (1518-1594): ARIADNE FOUND BY BACCHUS AND CROWNED BY VENUS.
1578. PAINTING ON CANVAS. SALA DELL'ANTICOLLEGIO, DUCAL PALACE.

Ordered by the Venetian government for the Salotto Quadrato in the Ducal Palace, these four large allegorical paintings (pages 184-187) were finished in 1578. In July of that year Paolo Veronese and Palma Giovane were called in to appraise them, and in November Tintoretto accordingly received fifty ducats (probably equivalent to about one thousand dollars) for each picture. These nudes rank among the finest figure paintings of Tintoretto's maturity.

TINTORETTO (1518-1594): MINERVA PROTECTING PEACE AND PLENTY AND REPELLING MARS. 1578.
PAINTING ON CANVAS. SALA DELL'ANTICOLLEGIO, DUCAL PALACE.

The original commission for these four paintings still exists and shows that they were intended to form an integral whole allegorically representing Union. In 1716, along with Veronese's *Rape of Europa* and Bassano's *Return of Jacob to Canaan* (reproduced on page 188), they were installed in the Sala dell'Anticollegio of the Ducal Palace, a room rebuilt by Palladio after the fire of 1574 and decorated with carvings and stuccoes by Alessandro Vittoria.

VIEW OF THE SALA DELL'ANTICOLLEGIO IN
THE DUCAL PALACE, WITH TINTORETTO'S
ALLEGORICAL PAINTINGS. LEFT, VULCAN WITH
THE CYCLOPES AT THE FORGE. RIGHT,
MERCURY WITH THE THREE GRACES.

ment concerning the proud Titian: "Only by that little flicker of light which he discerned in the things of Giorgione did he see and conceive the idea of painting perfectly."
And since that "little flicker of light" proved to be nothing short of a revelation, he
turned his back on everything he had previously learned. The new age of modern
painting thus began: the discovery of a rich and surging colour, full of mysterious
assonances, was well in keeping with Titian's dynamic composition, his full-bodied
forms and his free-ranging genius.

Tintoretto was a painter of a very different temperament, one who believed more in
visions and dreams than in reality. He was a prey all his life to spiritual conflicts
which break out and rise to their climax in violent clashes of light and shade. Titian
would have liked to stand without a rival in all the courts of Europe, to be the first

JACOPO BASSANO (1510-1592): THE RETURN OF JACOB TO CANAAN. PAINTING ON CANVAS. SALA DELL'ANTICOLLEGIO, DUCAL PALACE.

and only painter of the world. Tintoretto had no such ambitions. He was content with Venice, where he was born and where he spent every day of his life. When orders came to him from abroad, he had no compunction about sending the handiwork of his pupils, however inferior it might be to the standards he set himself. The best of his own work he reserved for Venice, for its finest and most famous buildings, for the Doge's Palace above all. There is not a room or anteroom in the Palace in which his genius is unrepresented; and we see him at his best in the four mythological paintings in the Anticollegio and, in the Hall of the Great Council, the vast *Glory of Paradise*, which Ruskin called "the most wonderful piece of pure, manly, and masterly oil painting in the world."

Ridolfi helps us to understand the ideas the artist had in mind when he conceived the paintings in the Anticollegio (the antechamber where illustrious persons waited before being ushered into the Doge's presence). They are described as follows in the order commissioning the work to be done: *"Vulcan with the Cyclopes at the Forge, The Three Graces, Minerva embracing Peace and Plenty and repelling Mars*, and *Ariadne with Bacchus in the Presence of Venus*, which together betoken Union." The Cyclopes, each in turn hammering the iron on the anvil to give it the desired shape, symbolize the union and concord of the Senators in the administration of the Republic. The weapons represented around them allude to the military preparedness of the Venetian State; weapons also served as ornaments of the city and as a stern warning to its enemies. The Graces correspond to the offices; one is leaning on a cube, while the other two are holding the myrtle and the sacred rose of Venus. They are accompanied by Mercury, for the "graces" vouchsafed by the State should be bestowed with discrimination. The prince who recognizes virtue and rewards services loyally rendered is to be likened to God, who does not leave good works unrequited. Minerva driving away Mars, while Peace and Plenty rejoice, alludes to the wisdom of the Republic which, by sparing them the ordeals of war, promotes the happiness of its subjects and teaches them to revere their leaders. Ariadne, found by Bacchus on the seashore and crowned by Venus who declares her free and admits her to the ranks of the gods, symbolizes Venice —Venice born on the seashore, blessed by God with every earthly boon, her brow encircled by a crown (i.e., liberty) bestowed by the gods, and her name inscribed in everlasting characters in the firmament.

This concept of union brings to mind the notion of "harmonic proportion" to which a French writer ascribed the beauty and power of Venice. It also recalls an observation of Francesco Sansovino: "From the union of the magistrates, who are joined together in an unexceptionably just proportion, derives the singular harmony which this admirable government perpetuates."

Tintoretto, it is not too much to say, left his spiritual autobiography in the series of fifty paintings in the Scuola Grande di San Rocco: from the prophetic visions of *Moses striking the Rock*, the *Plague of Serpents* and the *Fall of Manna*, to the mighty

TINTORETTO (1518-1594): ST MARY MAGDALEN. 1583-1587. PAINTING ON CANVAS.
SALA TERRENA, SCUOLA DI SAN ROCCO.

TINTORETTO (1518-1594): ST MARY OF EGYPT. 1583-1587. PAINTING ON CANVAS.
SALA TERRENA, SCUOLA DI SAN ROCCO.

MATTIA PAGAN. PROCESSION OF THE DOGE IN ST MARK'S SQUARE ON PALM

conception of *The Crucifixion* in the Sala dell'Albergo, to the storm-tossed leafage and running water, suddenly revealed in the glare of the lightning, in the paintings of *St Mary of Egypt* and *Mary Magdalen*—luminous figures quite unaffected by the angry and dramatic moods of nature.

By improving and cultivating her mainland holdings, Venice not only materially increased their value and her own resources, but also ensured the grateful allegiance of the local population. Even in the time of the war against the League of Cambrai, the countryfolk of Venetia remained staunchly loyal to Venice, opposing fierce resistance to the invading armies. When they had no arms with which to make a stand, they rolled stones and boulders down upon the passing troops from their hiding places in the mountains, then melted away, drawing the Emperor Maximilian up the valley of the Brenta in search of them. When the region was occupied by French and German troops, so many inhabitants were "robbed and killed," Machiavelli tells us, that one and all regretted the mild yoke of Venice and yearned to have their "first masters" back again. The League of Cambrai broke up and this was accomplished. Thereafter the clash of interests between city and country gradually ceased and the peasantry of Venetia came to play a necessary and recognized part in the material prosperity of the city. In the comedies of Ruzzante (1502?-1542) the peasant of that day does not speak in the gentle tones of an Arcadian shepherd, but with the violence and directness of a primitive being. "If I were to use the Tuscan language, I should feel as if I were spending the money of a foreign country," wrote one of the many authors

who, abandoning official, literary Italian, chose to spread and popularize the written use of the Venetian dialect, which has—so it is said—a raciness and expressive resources that even Tuscan cannot rival. The painting of Jacopo Bassano, showing humble countryfolk in their native Venetia even when the theme is ostensibly a Biblical one, is imbued with the same earthy realism.

Bassano gives expression to the mentality and the spiritual outlook of the people inhabiting the cities, the small market towns and the countryside of the North Italian mainland over which Venice had extended her hegemony in the fifteenth century. She ruled Verona, Padua, Bergamo, Brescia, Vicenza, Treviso, Belluno, Udine and Feltre. The Venetians, however, who had so much respect for their own past and who preferred to have allies rather than vassals, allowed most of these subject towns to govern themselves in accordance with their own ancient statutes. The Venetian occupation of this region, furthermore, left undisturbed the social structures and ways of life that had taken form in the Middle Ages, in the time of the free communes. And notwithstanding the progress accomplished under Venetian rule, peasant life continued to be marked, to an almost incredible degree, by a patriarchal simplicity and Biblical earthiness. The spirit of this life entered into the art of Jacopo Bassano, who was only superficially influenced by Humanism and the conquests of the Renaissance. In his pictures, alongside infiltrations of Renaissance culture, there accordingly persisted elements, forces and moods which had their origin in remote spiritual currents of the medieval world. Indeed, it is these very survivals that constitute the most novel and important feature of his work, for they enabled him to treat subjects and record aspects of daily life which an artist wholly devoted to Renaissance ideals would have either overlooked or ignored. In the seventeenth century, when there came an intense and profound renewal of religious feeling, it was natural that the painters who gave expression to that spiritual climate (like Velazquez and Georges de La Tour, not to mention the Flemish masters and some of the Italians) should have taken over from Bassano themes and inventions which he, in his own way, had rediscovered and imposed, such as the genre scene, the still life, landscape painting and, above all, scenes with nocturnal lighting effects.

It is an extraordinary spectacle, in studying the flowering of Venetian painting in the sixteenth century, to see two masters as dissimilar and antithetical as Tintoretto and Veronese working in Venice at the same time. In 1573 Veronese was summoned before the Tribunal of the Inquisition to answer the charge of taking irreverent liberties in the religious pictures he had painted. He replied that "we painters use the same licence as poets and madmen," and that it was idle to seek an underlying (i.e., heretical) intent in his paintings. These, he went on to say, represent only the things that the eye can see, every detail being chosen solely by virtue of its chromatic and formal values, and for no other reason. Have we here a plea in favour of pure art, of art for art's sake, to be judged solely by its decorative effect and the aesthetic enjoyment it procures? One is reminded of Lanzi's description of Veronese's *Triumph of Venice* on the ceiling of the Hall of the Great Council. "This picture is a compendium of all those wonderful touches by which Paolo delights the eye, confronting it with

MATTIA PAGAN. PROCESSION OF THE DOGE IN ST MARK'S SQUARE ON PALM SUNDAY, FRAGMENT. BETWEEN 1556 AND 1569. WOODCUT. MUSEO CORRER.

GIOVANNI BATTISTA BRUSTOLON (1712-1796): THE HALL OF THE GREAT COUNCIL IN THE DUCAL PALACE DURING A MEETING OF THE COUNCIL. ENGRAVING AFTER A PAINTING BY CANALETTO. MUSEO CORRER.

a concerted whole which casts a spell. Aerial spaces surpassingly bright and clear, palatial buildings that seem to lure one into them; joyful and noble faces for the most part painted from life and embellished with art; graceful, expressive movements, well contrasted; sumptuous garments, of the finest fabrics, beautifully cut; crowns, sceptres, wealth and magnificence worthy of so majestic a scene; objects shown in perspective recession; vivid colours and brushwork combining the utmost rapidity with a supreme control that at each touch acts, consummates and instructs." Here too, as in the sixteenth-century theatre, the public is intermingled with gods and goddesses and symbolic personages. In the Ducal Palace (Hall of the Great Council, Hall of the Council of Ten, Anticollegio, and Collegio) Veronese can be seen at his splendid best

In the fourteenth century the Hall of the Great Council was considerably enlarged, and in 1365 Guariento painted his *Paradise* on one of its walls. In the course of the next two centuries the Hall was decorated by Gentile da Fabriano, Pisanello, Gentile and Giovanni Bellini, Alvise Vivarini, Carpaccio, Titian, Pordenone, Veronese and Tintoretto. All these paintings were destroyed in the great fire of December 20, 1577. Veronese, Tintoretto, the Bassanos and others were then engaged to redecorate the Hall with scenes from Venetian history chosen by Gerolamo Bardi and Francesco Sansovino, advised by a committee of three Senators. By 1585 the paintings on the walls were finished, together with the thirty-five ceiling panels. In 1588-1590, on the vast wall behind the tribune, Tintoretto painted his *Glory of Paradise* to replace Guariento's ruined fresco.

VIEW OF THE HALL OF THE GREAT COUNCIL
IN THE DUCAL PALACE.

and his faculty of invention at its most brilliant. "We lift up our eyes to the ceiling, or rather up to Heaven," writes Boschini, "for these are truly celestial paintings, and fresher and lovelier than nature herself could have made them." From such easy perfection and serenity who would have guessed the troubles that were brewing in the outside world?

Ever since the political life of Italy had come to depend entirely on the moves of the two great rivals, the Emperor Charles V and the King of France, Venice had been taking an increasingly neutral view of international problems. In vain did the French ambassador invoke the past in order to bring the Venetians into the war against the Turks. When finally Venice decided to act, she only did so for imperative reasons of prestige, and she was not content with half-measures. In keeping with her pride and dignity she insisted on playing a leading part in the new crusade of Christendom against the Turk. At the great battle of Lepanto (October 7, 1571) the victorious Christian fleet numbered 214 vessels, 105 of them Venetian; of the 7637 soldiers and sailors killed, 4836 of them were Venetians. Such was the Serene Republic's contribution to victory—a victory, however, which did not yield the expected results.

Venice had been sorely tried by long and ruinous wars; her political and economic structure no longer had the elasticity of earlier times, nor the power of making good the heavy drains on her vitality. Henceforth, powerless to advance her interests by war, she began by degrees to assume a new character, indulging more and more in rhetorical gestures and self-exaltation. As one studies the paintings and decorations executed in the Ducal Palace after the fire of 1577, one is made aware of having crossed the later limits of the Renaissance and entered already the exuberant, triumphant world of the seventeenth century. Here once again she pointed the way to forms destined to be much imitated, but Venice has many faces and we must not be content with appearances. Spectacular superficialities there were in abundance in Venetian life of this age—receptions and entertainments, pomp and display, rhetoric and oratory. But there was dignity too and zeal in the public service. The nobleman on duty in the ports and strongholds of the Levant among hostile infidels, or in small garrison towns among insolent mercenaries, watching over the defence and welfare of Venice's colonial empire—this type of Venetian strikes a vivid contrast with the "simpering gentleman richly trimmed with lace in the Spanish manner, eaten up with self-conceit and dividing his time between love-making and duelling, of no use or profit either to himself or to others in the stately pomp of his palace" (Sestan). Yet Venice had the courage and determination to defy the pope in the time of the Interdict (1605-1607) and could still produce such admirable men as the great monk and theologian Fra Paolo Sarpi, a friend of Galileo's. So that the French historian Louvois, writing at the end of the seventeenth century, was only stating the truth when he observed that "although the Republic of Venice is today on the decline, she still retains much of her majesty."

PAOLO VERONESE (C. 1530-1588): THE TRIUMPH OF VENICE. 1584. CEILING PAINTING IN THE HALL OF THE GREAT COUNCIL, DUCAL PALACE. ▶

The Cabinet (Collegio), composed of the Doge and twenty-five Senators, met in the Sala del Collegio, and here foreign ambassadors were received. The design of the ceiling decoration, perhaps the most beautiful in the Ducal Palace, is attributed to Palladio. The gilded ornamental carving around the paintings is the work of Francesco Bello and Andrea Faentin and dates to 1577. The paintings themselves, seventeen in all, are by Paolo Veronese. The oval panel in the centre is an allegory of Faith, described in the motto beneath it as the Foundation of the Republic *(Reipubblicae Fundamentum)*. The central panel on the right represents Mars and Neptune,

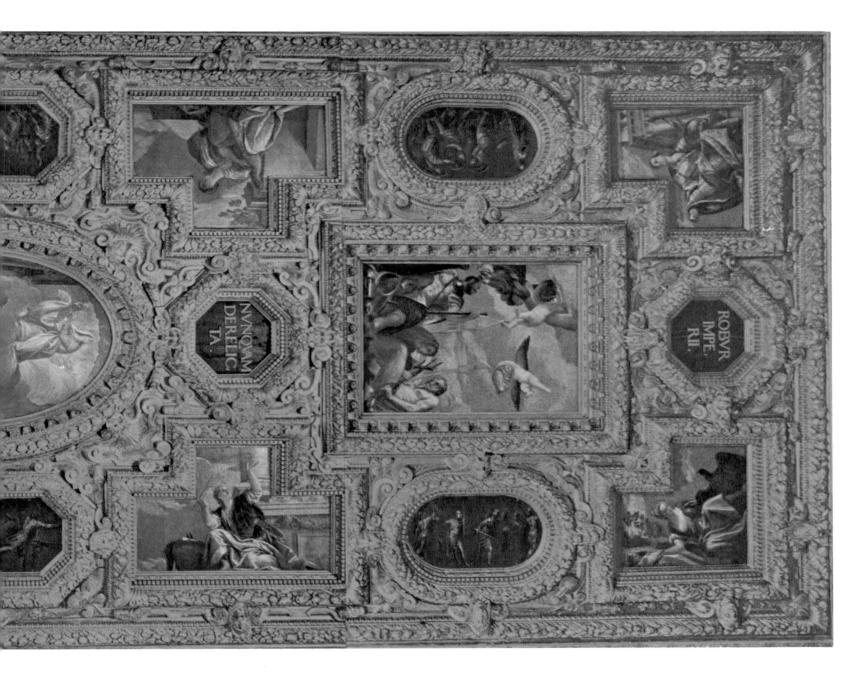

COLLEGIO IN THE DUCAL PALACE.

together symbolizing Venetian mastery of land and sea; the Campanile is visible in the background. The corresponding panel on the left represents Venice enthroned (with the Lion of St Mark lying quietly at her feet), honoured by Justice and Peace who are presenting her with a sword, an olive branch, and scales. The single allegorical figures grouped around them are Fidelity, Meekness (with her lamb), Dialectic, Recompense, Moderation, Simplicity, Vigilance, and Abundance. The small dark monochrome paintings, on historical and allegorical subjects, symbolize Good Government.

PAOLO VERONESE (C. 1530-1588): JUNO LAVISHING HER TREASURES ON VENICE. 1553-1554.
CEILING PAINTING IN THE HALL OF THE COUNCIL OF TEN, DUCAL PALACE.

GIOVANNI BATTISTA TIEPOLO (1696-1770): THE MARRIAGE OF NEPTUNE AND VENICE.
PAINTING ON CANVAS. QUADRERIA, DUCAL PALACE.

The age of Baroque culture in Venice is rich in great names in music, historiography and art criticism, while at the same time it witnessed some of the most characteristic diversions of Venetian life in the later, less glorious days of the Republic: the number of pageants and ceremonies increased with each passing year, and so did the number of theatres. By the middle of the seventeenth century there were sixteen opera theatres and playhouses in Venice, and the greatest painters of the day designed costumes and painted scenery for plays and pageants. More than ever the patrician families indulged the Venetian love of gorgeous display and lavish decorations, for which the best artists catered; and that love of display assumed even greater proportions after the great plague of 1629-1630, lasting sixteen months, when tens of thousands perished and wealth and property were left concentrated in the hands of a few. The demand for decorations and works of art was then so great, and the guilds had been so much depleted in the epidemic, that the government was compelled to admit foreign craftsmen and artists to membership in them.

Canaletto, Guardi and all the painters of the eighteenth century made a habit of placing the church of Santa Maria della Salute in the centre of their views of Venice, lingering over it as if it had been built by one of themselves. The art of their contemporary, Giovanni Battista Tiepolo, may well strike us as a kind of sequel to that of Paolo Veronese, and indeed there is no real break in continuity between Veronese and Tiepolo, for little had changed in the mood of Venice since the Peace of Bologna in 1529; thereafter, indeed, one century much resembles another.

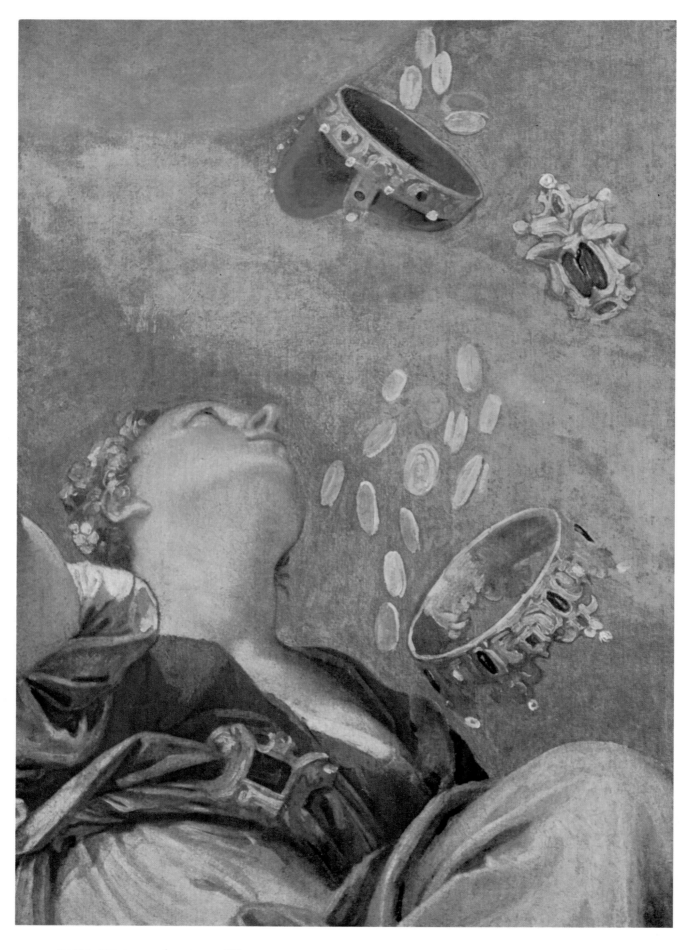

PAOLO VERONESE (C. 1530-1588): JUNO LAVISHING HER TREASURES ON VENICE, DETAIL. 1553-1554.
CEILING PAINTING IN THE HALL OF THE COUNCIL OF TEN, DUCAL PALACE.

The end of the seventeenth century witnessed the final phases of the struggle against the Turks. For centuries Venice had borne the brunt of the Turkish wars in defence of Christendom. Now the leadership of the Christian cause passed to the House of Austria and John Sobieski, in 1683, saved Vienna from the Turks, who were routed from the field. This triumph has been justly celebrated by historians and poets as much as, if not more than, the naval victory won at Lepanto. Encouraged by the Turkish repulse at Vienna, Venice embarked on a campaign of her own and her last great captain and Doge, Francesco Morosini, succeeded in reconquering the Morea (Peloponnese) in 1686-1687. But it was a brief triumph: by 1716 the Turks had won

GIOVANNI BATTISTA TIEPOLO (1696-1770): THE MARRIAGE OF NEPTUNE AND VENICE, DETAIL.
PAINTING ON CANVAS. QUADRERIA, DUCAL PALACE.

back the Morea. The days of conquest and empire were over, and for the rest of the eighteenth century, delivered from the heavy burdens of war, the Venetians lived in halcyon peace, enjoying a ceaseless round of revels and pageants. "The ancient myth, touching the almost proverbial wisdom of the Venetian government, now gave place to another: the myth of a peace-loving Republic, fruit of a peace which the glorious exertions of the elders had succeeded in securing for her" (Berengo).

Who can say whether, in Venice, the seventeenth and eighteenth centuries were an age of decadence or one of progress? The upper classes lived in greater luxury than ever. The production of works of art was on the increase. More and more new houses and palaces were being built, both in Venice and in Venetia. The number of domestic servants doubled, and so did the number of shops. The sale of municipal property —to meet military expenses in the earlier part of this period—brought 38.9% of the real estate thus disposed of into the hands of the nobility. The economic power and landed property of the patrician class were therefore steadily increasing, and consequently brought about an increased profusion and display in their style of living. In the fifteenth century the Venetian nobility accounted for 4.5% of the entire population; by 1791 that figure had fallen to 2.5%. This means that, as family after family died out, their property passed to those that survived, thus gradually concentrating wealth in the hands of a small number of grandees.

At this moment Giovanni Battista Tiepolo appeared on the scene—the perfect moment for an artist of his stamp. In the great palaces then being restored and redecorated, in the villas dotted along the banks of the Brenta and over the wooded slopes of Venetia, in the churches where eighteenth-century taste called for colourful decorations, Tiepolo for fifty years lavished the inexhaustible resources of his pictorial imagination. And as if this were not enough, he found time, working as he did with unbelievable ease and speed, to respond to the invitations of foreign princes, who were eager to secure his services for the glory of their house. The secret of his popularity lies in the wealth and exuberance of his imagination, and even more in the fluency and felicity of his brushwork.

The unexampled ease and sweep of Tiepolo's handling are the cumulative outcome and final fruit not only of the Cinquecento tradition but of all the inventions and discoveries of the Baroque age. He had a notable predecessor in Gian Antonio Pellegrini, who in travelling all over Europe and studying the best Roman, Neapolitan and Flemish masters, had introduced into Venetian painting what was to be its most celebrated characteristic: a luminous and soaring brio, genial and buoyant, brooking no restraint. Nor was this happy and spirited ease of manner the prerogative of painters alone; the music and sculpture of eighteenth-century Venice, even the furniture, the blown glass, the books and engravings of the period, all reveal the exquisite elegance and refined taste of a unitary civilization still in the afterglow of its heyday.

GIOVANNI BATTISTA TIEPOLO (1696-1770): TRIUMPH OF THE PISANI FAMILY. 1761.
CEILING PAINTING IN THE BALL ROOM OF THE VILLA PISANI AT STRA, ON THE BRENTA.

GIOVANNI BATTISTA TIEPOLO (1696-1770): INDIANS PERSONIFYING AMERICA, DETAIL OF THE TRIUMPH OF THE PISANI FAMILY. 1761.
CEILING PAINTING IN THE BALL ROOM OF THE VILLA PISANI AT STRA, ON THE BRENTA.

In the great ceiling decoration of the Villa Pisani at Stra, Tiepolo represented the triumph of the House of Pisani. "In the centre of the fresco," writes Gallo, "is the Virgin seated amid the clouds, surrounded by angels and the theological virtues, Faith, Hope and Charity, together with Wisdom, who is reading a large book. Below is the majestic figure of a woman, personifying the mother country, with a turreted crown on her head and in her hand a sceptre ending in a cross; she is looking up towards the Virgin to invoke her blessing and protection on behalf of the Pisani. And while Almorò Pisani II, called Andrea, remains somewhat to one side (in token of the fact that he was already dead), his son Almorò, a young boy shown in the act of painting, and dressed in blue, is seated in the lap of his mother Marina Sagredo, personifying Art. This group is surrounded by the Arts and Sciences and the Four Parts of the World protected by Peace and Plenty holding in their hands green olive branches and laurel wreaths."

No one surpassed the Venetians in interpreting the ambitious dreams and celebrating the past glories of princely dynasties and noble families. Though there was not always a Giovanni Battista Tiepolo available to answer the call and proceed to Würzburg or the court of Spain, Venice never lacked for painters capable of conjuring up populous triumphs and ready to fresco vast wall spaces in France or England or wherever they might be called. Decorative painting on historical themes, this was the great speciality of the Venetians and opened the way to the diffusion of their art abroad. As they came in contact with Transalpine forms and adjusted their work to the requirements of the wealthier nations of Europe, Venetian painters spread and popularized the genre scene, the *veduta*, and landscape painting. It was just about this time, as it so happened, that the Dutch school was on the decline, and its slackening production no longer sufficed to meet the demands of English collectors. Venetian painters, attracted by English wealth, stepped into the breach and turned their hands to various types of painting which they had hitherto neglected, but for which there was now a market—fruit and flower pictures, views and landscapes of fantasy, all increasingly in demand. Venetian gazettes published articles translated from the Dutch; Goldoni introduced Dutchmen into his comedies; publishing activities stimulated the rivalry between Venice and Amsterdam; the music of Vivaldi and other Italian composers was more frequently published in Holland than in Venice. By exporting works of art and catering for foreign collectors Venetian painters brought about a revival of the arts in Venice.

Christian Cole and Joseph Smith, the British Consul, two of the most avid collectors of Venetian paintings, came to assume an almost directorial position in the art world of eighteenth-century Venice. The first persuaded Rosalba Carriera to devote herself to pastels and invited to England Gian Antonio Pellegrini and Marco Ricci. The second brought together a famous collection of masterpieces and was "the friend and patron of Canaletto, for whom he acted for nearly twenty-five years as business manager" (Francis Henry Taylor). Moreover, the travels of Venetian artists over the length and breadth of Europe, and the long stays they made in foreign capitals and the seats of English lords, inevitably affected both their outlook and their style; many aspects of Settecento Venetian painting can be understood only in the light of these foreign contacts. Giovanni Battista Piazzetta, when not painting sacred works, specialized in imaginative portraits of plebeian characters and scenes of rustic life which are in many ways reminiscent of Terbrugghen. Other artists, in their paintings, drawings and engravings, went to Rembrandt, Willem van de Velde and Jan van Goyen for inspiration.

Pietro Longhi, after trying his hand at fresco painting in his youth, wisely gave it up and specialized in genre painting. Longhi represents a particular aspect of Venetian life, and in a way that marks a sharp and undisguised break with the Venetian tradition. Large-scale compositions were ill suited to his peculiar genius which, like that of

BALDASSARE LONGHENA (1598-1682): THE CHURCH OF SANTA MARIA DELLA SALUTE ON THE GRAND CANAL. BUILT BETWEEN 1631 AND 1681.

The construction of the great church of Santa Maria della Salute on the Grand Canal, commissioned by the government to commemorate the deliverance of Venice from the plague (October 22, 1630), was entrusted to Baldassare Longhena. In designing the building, he gave a new interpretation of the domes of St Mark's and magnified, to the highest degree, those effects of showy pomp and scenic perspective of which Venetians are so fond. Here he created the one indubitable masterpiece of seventeenth-century Venetian art, taking inspiration from the "rounded structures" with acrobats and fireworks which, during festivities and celebrations, were drawn by boats over the waters of the Lagoon or erected in the Piazzetta, as shown below in Guardi's painting.

FRANCESCO GUARDI (1712-1793): FESTIVITIES IN THE PIAZZETTA ON THE LAST THURSDAY OF CARNIVAL. LOUVRE, PARIS.

CANALETTO (1697-1768): THE FEAST OF THE ASCENSION, SHOWING THE BUCENTAUR IN FRONT OF THE DUCAL PALACE AND THE PIAZZETTA. ALDO CRESPI COLLECTION, MILAN.

Goldoni, led him to record some of the more intimate and diverting aspects of eighteenth-century life. His patrons did not expect him to concoct elaborate allegories in celebration of past triumphs flattering to family pride. It was enough for them that he should give them a memento of a particular event of family life or recount an episode which it would be pleasant or amusing to look back upon. The ancient bourgeoisie, which had done so much for the prosperity and well-being of Venice, found at last, in Longhi, a painter after its own heart.

Andrea Tron, Inquisitor of the Arts in 1781, declared to the Senate that "if the rich, given over to soft and luxurious living, were not to play their part again, as they had in the past, in commerce, the arts and navigation, there could be no hope left for the Republic." But it was useless to appeal to the public spirit. That spirit was dead; the decline was too far advanced for there to be any hope of arresting it. As her trade languished and she retired from the political scene, Venice gradually became the playground of Europe. Even so, she could still on occasion nurse the illusion that the receptions and entertainments provided for foreign princes might be the flattering prelude to political agreements—but those princes, in coming to Venice, were bent only on pleasure and amusement. Great nobles representing the Republic abroad, and the great patrician families at home, squandered fortunes on revels and entertainments, vying with each other in ruinous ostentation while the government strove to outdo them all and show the world that the pride and glory of the ancient Republic of Venice were still undimmed. So it was that in the eighteenth century, when her effective power was shorn away, her State ceremonies and public shows achieved a splendour and magnificence beyond all precedent. The ancient ceremonial, Byzantine

FRANCESCO GUARDI (1712-1793): THE DOGE IN THE BUCENTAUR LEAVING FOR THE LIDO TO CELEBRATE THE ANNUAL WEDDING OF THE SEA. LOUVRE, PARIS.

FRANCESCO GUARDI (1712-1793): CONSECRATION OF THE DOGE IN ST MARK'S. MUSÉE ROYAL DES BEAUX-ARTS, BRUSSELS.

The election of a new Doge set in motion a whole train of ceremonies and festivities. His election was announced by a volley of cannon fired from a galley anchored in the Lagoon, while church bells rang all over the city. A deputation of six magistrates proceeded to the home of the newly elected Doge, announced the news to him, and escorted him to the Ducal Palace. From there he was conducted into St Mark's where, from the marble pulpit to the right of the choir, he was presented to the people. Mass was then celebrated, after which the new Doge swore to abide by the laws of the State.

FRANCESCO GUARDI (1712-1793): THE DOGE CARRIED IN TRIUMPH ROUND ST MARK'S SQUARE. MUSÉE DE PEINTURE ET SCULPTURE, GRENOBLE.

Receiving the banner of the Republic from the Primicerius, the leading ecclesiastic of the city, and being draped in the ducal cloak, the new Doge left the church and stepped into the *pozzetto*, a wooden tribune in which he was carried in triumph round the square by twenty seamen from the Arsenal. Another contingent of Arsenal men, armed with long staffs, held back the crowd. The Admiral of the Venetian fleet stood behind him, holding the banner, while the Doge threw to the people the gold and silver coins, bearing his effigy, which had been struck at the mint during the previous night.

FRANCESCO GUARDI (1712-1793): CORONATION OF THE DOGE ON THE GIANTS' STAIRCASE. LOUVRE, PARIS.

After being consecrated in the church and acclaimed by the people in St Mark's Square, the new Doge proceeded to the Ducal Palace. Passing through the Porta della Carta and the Arco Foscari, he mounted the Giants' Staircase, expressly built to give increased solemnity to the ceremony, which the people crowded into the courtyard to witness. At the top of the stairs, between Sansovino's gigantic statues of Mars and Neptune, the coronation ceremony took place: the horned cap was placed on his head while the oldest Senator pronounced the sacramental words, "Receive the crown of the Dukedom of Venice."

in origin, lost the hieratic gravity and stateliness of old; it now gave rise to pageantry unbelievably costly and spectacular, regattas, receptions, annual fairs and carnivals, and the periodic coronation of the Doge—so many pretexts for carefree excitement and public gaiety in which all took part, from the highest to the lowest.

The charm, the amenity, the décor of Venetian life became proverbial throughout Europe, and painters were in demand as never before to portray the city in its most characteristic and suggestive moods and aspects. In the paintings of Canaletto, the heroic vision dear to the sixteenth- and seventeenth-century masters and still maintained by Tiepolo was broken up into the innumerable, delicately assembled elements that go to make up his canals and piazzas, his views of the Lagoon, their light and movement subtly changing with the time of year. Figures and buildings seem to shimmer in tremulous masses of air as clear as crystal, quickened by the vivid, glancing colours of a holiday atmosphere.

Yet, if we look beneath the surface animation of these incomparably fresh and appealing views of eighteenth-century Venice and take the trouble to analyze this concluding chapter in the history of the city, we find, as often as not, an underlying melancholy, a pervading sense of desolation and nostalgia.

Venice had long since lost her ancient, privileged position as a great emporium on the main trade route between Europe and the East, and had declined, as Fanfani writes, to the level of a local port serving her metropolitan and colonial possessions. Once the marketplace of the world, Venice now did most of her business in the heavy atmosphere of her ridottos and gambling dens. The Venetian aristocracy was swept along with the current—swept too far and too fast for there to be any hope of renewal or reform. There was no turning back. Intent on remaining in power at all costs and preserving their privileges, they spent freely and lived gaily with little thought for the morrow.

Giovanni Battista Tiepolo, befriended and patronized by the nobles, and famous above all for his splendid frescoes glorifying his noble patrons, in fact drew monsters and caricatures in secret. The most brilliant masters of the Rococo, Francesco Guardi, for example, for all the lightness and charm of their touch, verge at times on the harsh and expressionistic; figures tend to become mere coloured shapes, as elusive and unsubstantial as dead leaves. Yet no painter has better conveyed the Venetian atmosphere than Guardi—an atmosphere pervaded by reflected light and broken gleams, echoing as with the sound of voices. With the delicate tones and flickering linework of his best views of the city and the lagoons, the great age of Venetian painting comes to a close. In Venice as in Spain, the two most conservative nations of eighteenth-century Europe, the nobility hastened to its ruin and downfall, followed in Venice by the ironic gaze of Gian Domenico Tiepolo, in Spain by the implacable sarcasms of Goya.

PIETRO LONGHI (1702-1785): SCENE WITH MASKED FIGURES. PAINTING ON CANVAS. CA' REZZONICO, VENICE.

Paolo Renier, the one hundred and nineteenth Doge of Venice, died on February 18, 1789, in the middle of Carnival week. In order not to disturb the merry-making, he was buried without much ceremony and the news was kept secret for ten days. He was succeeded by Lodovico Manin, the last of Venice's one hundred and twenty Doges. On May 12, 1797, as the troops of General Bonaparte were marching towards the Lagoon, the Great Council met for the last time. "As we were about to deliberate," wrote Manin in his Memoirs, "a discharge of musketry was heard which caused much alarm among us, and the patricians rushed to the doors. . ." The meeting broke up.

GIOVANNI DOMENICO TIEPOLO (1727-1804): THE SPRING SHOWER. PEN AND WASH DRAWING IN SEPIA. THE CLEVELAND MUSEUM OF ART, PURCHASE FROM THE J.H. WADE FUND.

In vain did the crowd in the square below cheer for the ancient Republic to the cry of "Viva San Marco!" In vain did many of them take up arms in its defence. In a day or two Bonaparte was master of the city. The thousand-year history of the great Republic of Venice had come to an end.

Confined to the islands of the Lagoon, her days of power and empire but a fading memory, the city seemed doomed to neglect and oblivion, but some of the leading spirits of Europe came one by one under the spell of her history and her beauty.

Byron, Turner, Corot, Musset, George Sand, Ruskin and Henri de Régnier are among those who rediscovered Venice. The Impressionists were fascinated by her light and her colours shimmering in the water. After them came Thomas Mann, Proust, Simmel, Kokoschka. The perennial attraction of Venice is perhaps greater today than it has ever been. Her visitors come from all over the world, and to all she offers unstintingly the accumulated treasures of her past, the serene profusion of her man-made and her natural beauties—a city which, wrested from the sea by human hands, must now be one of the last in the world to keep to the due measure of man's needs.

BIBLIOGRAPHY

ARETINO, P. *I libri delle lettere*, Paris 1608-1609.

BARDI, G. *Dichiarazione di tutte historie...*, Venice 1585.

BATTISTELLA, A. *La repubblica di Venezia nei suoi undici secoli di storia*, Venice 1921.

BERENGO, M. *La società veneta alla fine del Settecento*, Florence 1956.

BERENSON, B. *The Italian Painters of the Renaissance*, London 1952.

BETTINI, S. *Mosaici antichi di San Marco a Venezia*, Bergamo 1944.

BOSCHINI, M. *Le Ricche Minere*, Venice 1674.

BROWN, H. F. *Venetian Studies*, London 1887.

BROWN, H. F. *Venice, An Historical Sketch of the Republic*, London 1895.

CANAL, M. da. *La Cronaca dei Veneziani*, edited by A. Rossi. Archivio Storico Italiano, 1945.

CECCHETTI, B. *Il Doge di Venezia*, Venice 1864.

CESSI, R. *Storia della Repubblica di Venezia*, Milan 1946.

CIPOLLA, C. M. *Monete e civiltà mediterranea*, Venice 1957.

COLONNA, F. *Hypnerotomachia Polyphili*, Venice 1499.

COMMYNES, P. de. *Mémoires de Philippe de Commynes*, edited by Bernard de Mandrot, Paris 1901-1903.

CROWE and CAVALCASELLE, *Life and Times of Titian*, London 1877.

DAVIS, J. C. *The Decline of the Venetian Nobility as a Ruling Class*, Baltimore 1962.

DEMUS, O. *Die Mosaiken von San Marco in Venedig*, Vienna 1935.

DEMUS, O. *Die Reliefikonen der Westfassade von San Marco.* Lehrbuch der Öst. Byzantinischen Geschichte, III, 1959.

DEMUS, O. *The Church of San Marco in Venice. History, Architecture, Sculpture*, Washington 1960.

DOLCE, L. *Dialogo della pittura*, Venice 1557.

ESCHER, K. *Die Gemälde im Dogenpalast und ihre Bedeutung für das Barock*, Repertorium für Kunstwissenschaft, XLI, 1919.

FIOCCO, G. *L'arte di Andrea Mantegna*, Venice 1959.

FOSCARINI, M. *Della letteratura veneziana*, Venice 1854.

GALLO, R. *I Pisani e i palazzi di S. Stefano e di Stra*, Venice 1945.

GIANNOTTI, D. *Libro de la republica de Vinitiani*, Rome 1540.

GRABAR, A. *Byzance et Venise*, in *Venezia e l'Europa*, Venice 1956.

GUGLIELMO PUGLIESE. *Gesta Roberti Viscardi*, Germ. Hist. Script., IX, pp. 239-298.

HADELN, D. von. *La "Venetia" del Sansovino come fonte per la storia della pittura veneziana.* Jahrbuch der preussischen Kunstsammlungen, XXXI, 1910.

HADELN, D. von. *Beiträge zur Geschichte des Dogenpalastes.* Jahrbuch der preussischen Kunstsammlungen, XXXII, 1911.

JOHN THE DEACON (JOHANNES DIACONUS). *Chronica*, edited by C. Monticolo. Fonti per la Storia d'Italia, Rome 1890.

KRETSCHMAYR, H. *Geschichte von Venedig*, Stuttgart 1934.

LANZI, L. *Storia pittorica dell'Italia*, Bassano 1837-1839.

LEMAIRE DE BELGES, J. *Œuvres complètes*, Louvain 1882.

LENGHERAND, G. *Voyages... (1485-1486)*, Mons 1861.

LEVI, C. A. *Le collezioni veneziane d'arte e d'antichità dal secolo XIV ai nostri giorni*, Venice 1900.

LORENZETTI, G. *Venezia e il suo estuario*, Rome 1956.

LORENZI, G. B. *Monumenti per servire alla storia del Palazzo Ducale*, Venice 1961.

LOUVOIS, F. M. *Histoire du gouvernement de Venise*, Amsterdam 1695.

LUZZATO, G. *Storia economica di Venezia dall'XI al XVI secolo*, Venice 1961.

MALIPIERO, D. *Annali veneti*, edited by Longo, Rome 1843.

MANETTI, Z. M. *Specchio della giustizia*, Venice 1530.

MANUZIO, P. *Lettera ad Andrea Loredan (1552)*, Venice 1560.

MEDIN, A. *La storia della repubblica di Venezia nella poesia*, Milan 1904.

MICHIEL, M. A. *Notizie d'opere di disegno*, Bologna 1884.

MOLMENTI, P. *La storia di Venezia nella vita privata*, Bergamo 1904.

MONTICOLO, G. *Cronache veneziane antichissime*, Rome 1890.

MOSTO, A. da. *I Dogi di Venezia*, Venice 1939.

NANI, B. *Historia della Repubblica veneta*, Bologna 1680.

PANOFSKY, E. *Studies in Iconology*, New York 1939.

PAOLETTI, P. *L'architettura e la scultura del Rinascimento a Venezia*, Venice 1893.

PIRENNE, H. *Economic and Social History of Medieval Europe*, London 1949.

PRIULI, G. *I Diarii*, edited by R. Cessi, Bologna 1936.

RAVÀ, B. *Venise dans la littérature française*, Paris 1916.

RIDOLFI, C. *Le maraviglie dell'arte*, Venice 1648.

ROMANIN, S. *Storia documentata di Venezia*, Venice 1858.

RUSKIN, J. *Works*, edited by Cook and Wedderburn: Vols. IX-XI, *The Stones of Venice*, and Vol. XXIV, *St Mark's Rest*, London 1906.

SABELLICO, M. A. *Historia Venitiana*, Venice 1558.

SAGREDO, A. *Sulle consorterie delle arti edificatorie in Venezia*, Venice 1856.

SANUDO, M. *Le vite dei Dogi*, edited by G. Monticolo, Città di Castello 1920.

SANSOVINO, F. *Venetia città Nobilissima et singolare*, edited by Martinioni, Venice 1663.

SCHMARSOW, A. *Der Dogenpalast*, Repertorium für Kunstwissenschaft, XVIII, 1895.

SCHRAMM, P. E. *Herrschaftszeichen und Staatssymbolik*, Stuttgart 1954-1956.

STEFANINI, L. *Il motivo della "Tempesta" di Giorgione*, Padua 1955.

Storia della Civiltà Veneziana, a series of studies published by the Centro di Cultura e Civiltà, Cini Foundation, Venice (1955-1961), including writings by the following scholars: L. COLETTI, R. MOROZZO DELLA ROCCA, F. BABINGER, B. NARDI, F. CHABOD, G. BARBLAN, F. BRAUDEL, H. JEDIN, W. T. ELWERT, G. FIOCCO, E. SESTAN, N. IVANOFF, A. FANFANI, M. BERENGO, A. CHASTEL.

SWOBODA, R. W. *Römische und Romanische Paläste*, Vienna 1924.

TAYLOR, F. H. *The Taste of Angels*, Boston 1948.

VASARI, G. *Le vite de' più eccellenti architetti, pittori et scultori italiani*, second edition, Florence 1568.

VENTURI, L. *Giorgione e il giorgionismo*, Milan 1913.

WICKHOFF, F. *Der Saal des Grossen Rates zu Venedig*, Repertorium für Kunstwissenschaft, VI, 1883.

ZANOTTO, F. *Il Palazzo Ducale di Venezia illustrato*, Venice 1842-1861.

ZOVENZONI, R. *La vita e i carmi*, edited by Biliotto, Trieste 1950.

GENERAL INDEX

LIST OF ILLUSTRATIONS